Contents

Use the blocks to add.

4 + 1 = __5__	2 + 3 = ______
1 + 1 = ______	2 + 2 = ______
1 + 4 = ______	3 + 2 = ______
3 + 1 = ______	1 + 2 = ______
1 + 3 = ______	2 + 1 = ______

Draw s to help you add.

● ●●

$1 + 2 = \underline{\ \ 3\ \ }$

$2 + 3 = \underline{\hphantom{xxxx}}$

$3 + 1 = \underline{\hphantom{xxxx}}$

$1 + 4 = \underline{\hphantom{xxxx}}$

$1 + 3 = \underline{\hphantom{xxxx}}$

$2 + 1 = \underline{\hphantom{xxxx}}$

$2 + 2 = \underline{\hphantom{xxxx}}$

$1 + 1 = \underline{\hphantom{xxxx}}$

$3 + 2 = \underline{\hphantom{xxxx}}$

$4 + 1 = \underline{\hphantom{xxxx}}$

Sums to 5

Use the key to color the picture.

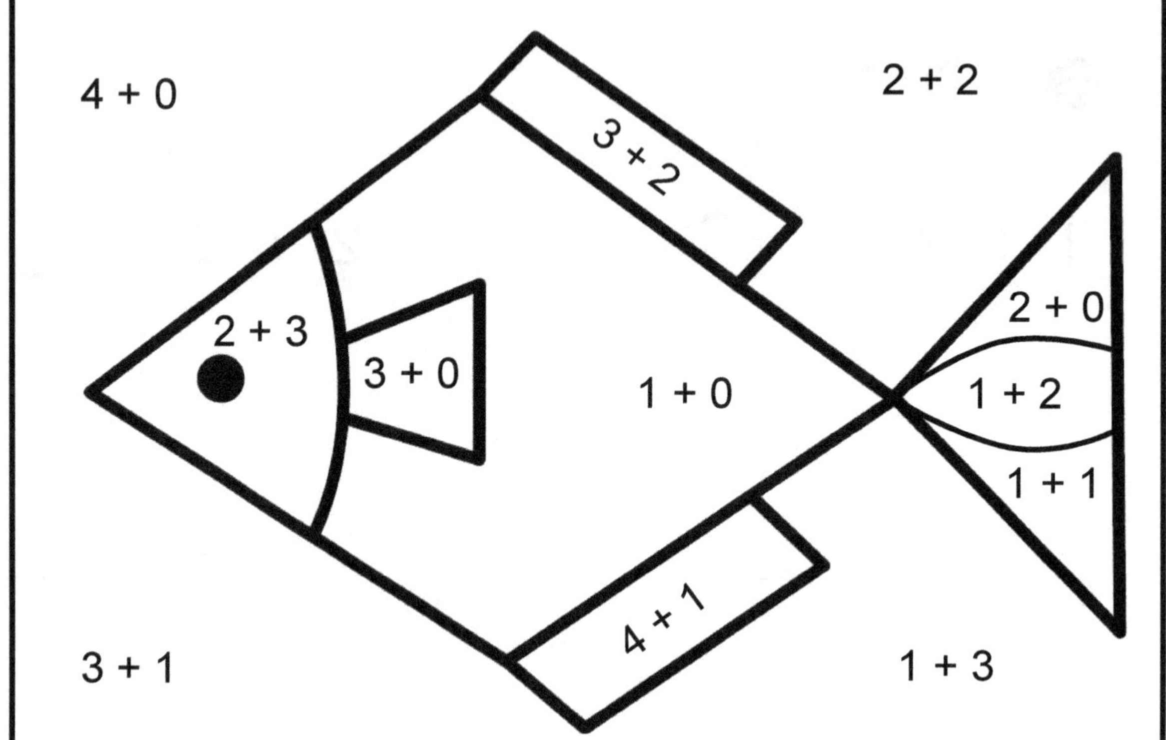

Complete the sums.

4 + 1 = _____	3 + 1 = _____	1 + 1 = _____
2 + 0 = _____	5 + 0 = _____	2 + 3 = _____
1 + 3 = _____	0 + 1 = _____	0 + 5 = _____
2 + 2 = _____	1 + 4 = _____	2 + 1 = _____
1 + 0 = _____	3 + 2 = _____	4 + 0 = _____
0 + 4 = _____	1 + 2 = _____	0 + 2 = _____

Addition Facts for 2, 3, 4, and 5

Use the key to color the picture.

Color Key
2 – red
3 – blue
4 – green
5 – yellow

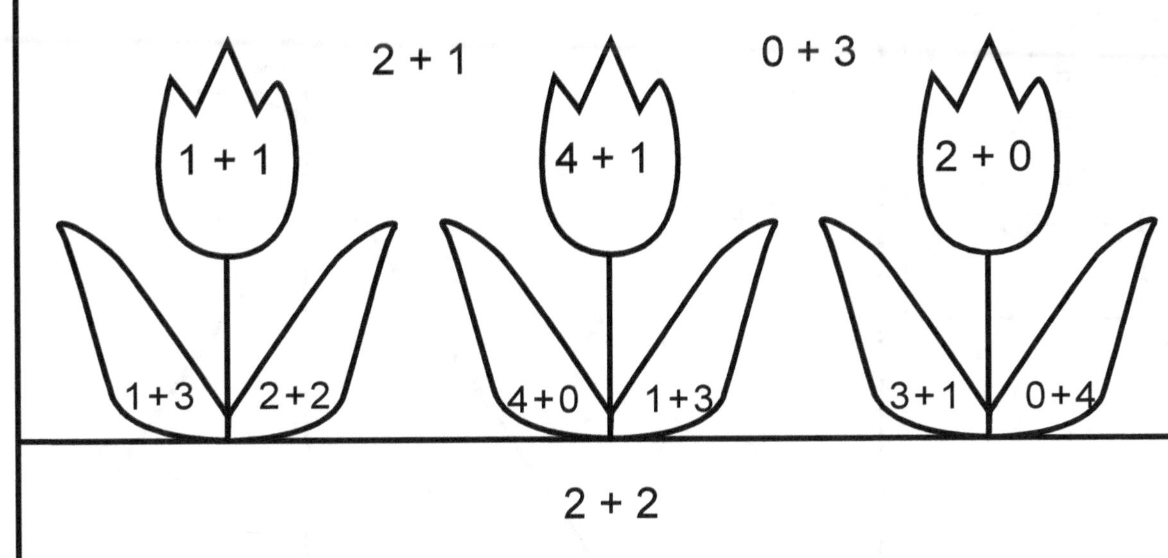

Complete the facts.

0 + 5 = ___	1 + 1 = ___	4 + 0 = ___
1 + 2 = ___	4 + 1 = ___	2 + 0 = ___
1 + 4 = ___	0 + 4 = ___	2 + 3 = ___
0 + 3 = ___	2 + 2 = ___	0 + 2 = ___
3 + 2 = ___	3 + 1 = ___	5 + 0 = ___
2 + 1 = ___	1 + 3 = ___	3 + 0 = ___

Use the key to color the picture.

Color Key
6 – red
7 – blue
8 – green
9 – yellow

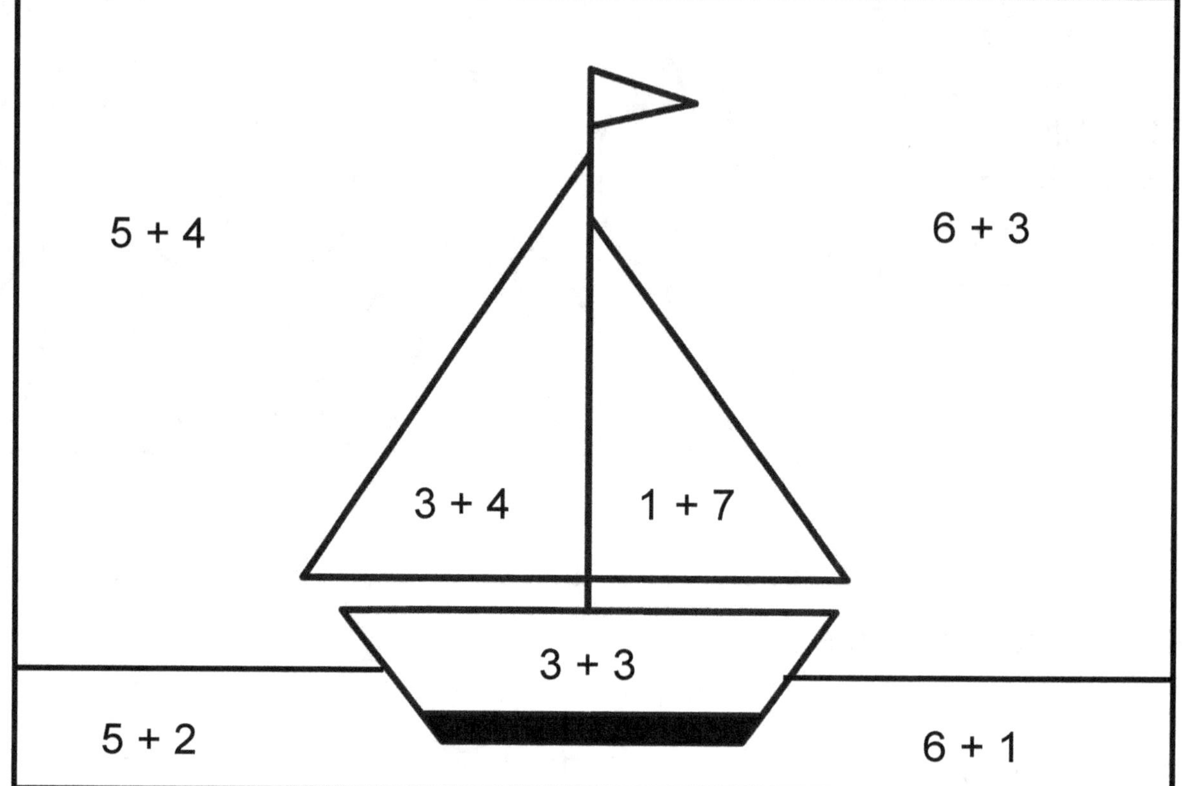

Complete the facts.

1 + 5 = ___   2 + 6 = ___   3 + 4 = ___

0 + 9 = ___   2 + 5 = ___   0 + 8 = ___

1 + 7 = ___   4 + 5 = ___   2 + 7 = ___

0 + 6 = ___   3 + 5 = ___   0 + 7 = ___

1 + 6 = ___   3 + 3 = ___   4 + 4 = ___

4 + 2 = ___   1 + 8 = ___   2 + 4 = ___

How Many Ways Can You Make 10?

Use the ten frames to make 10. Use two different colors. Then, write the answers.

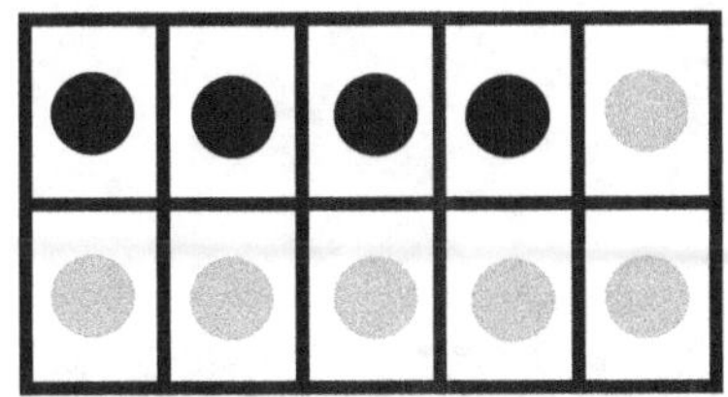

$$\underline{\quad 4 \quad} + \underline{\quad 6 \quad} = \underline{\quad 10 \quad}$$

$$\underline{\qquad} + \underline{\qquad} = \underline{\qquad}$$

$$\underline{\qquad} + \underline{\qquad} = \underline{\qquad}$$

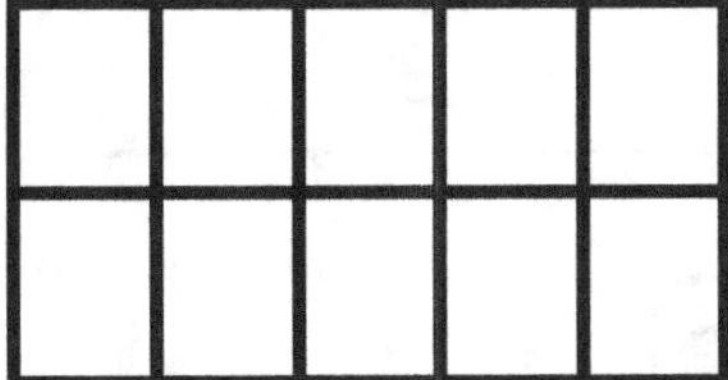

$$\underline{\qquad} + \underline{\qquad} = \underline{\qquad}$$

$$\underline{\qquad} + \underline{\qquad} = \underline{\qquad}$$

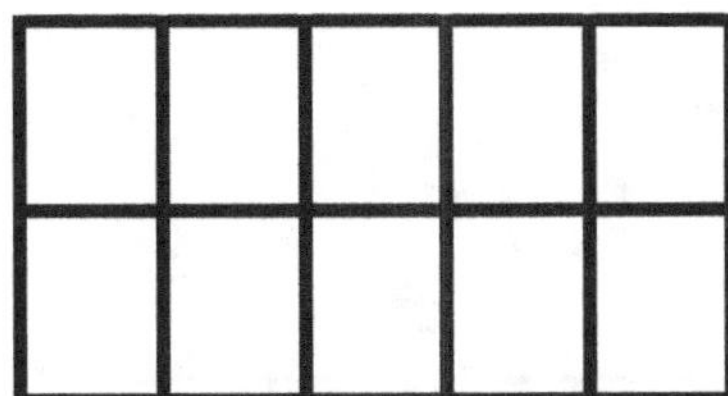

$$\underline{\qquad} + \underline{\qquad} = \underline{\qquad}$$

Addition Practice—Sums to 10

Write the number sentence.

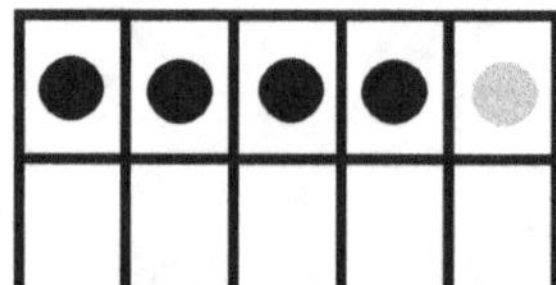

$$4 + 1 = 5$$

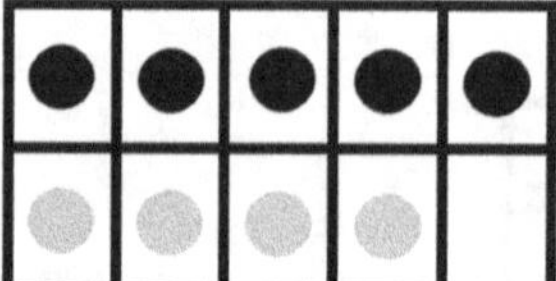

______ + ______ = ______

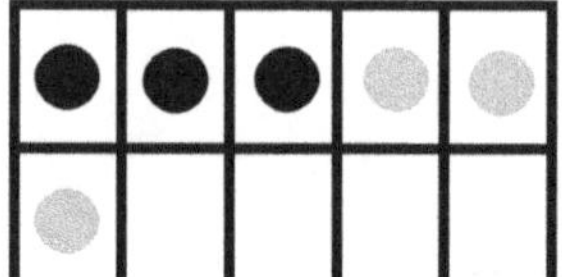

______ + ______ = ______

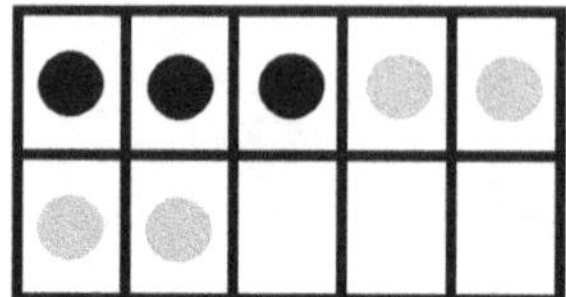

______ + ______ = ______

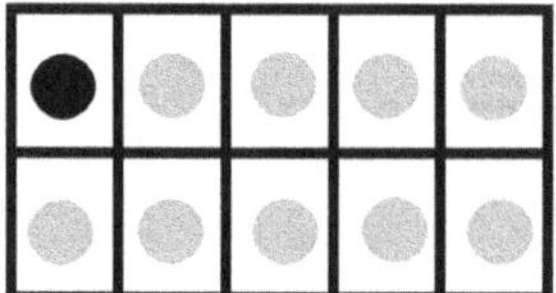

______ + ______ = ______

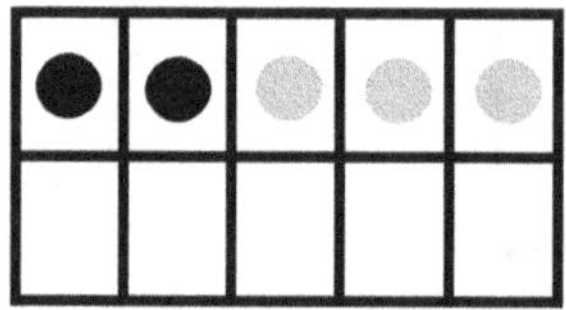

______ + ______ = ______

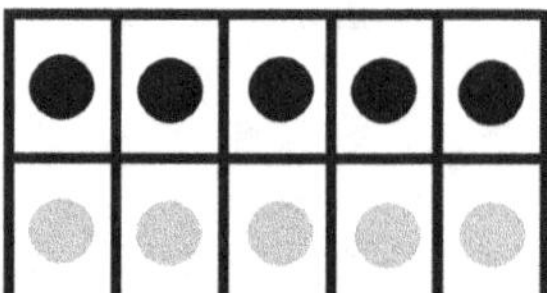

______ + ______ = ______

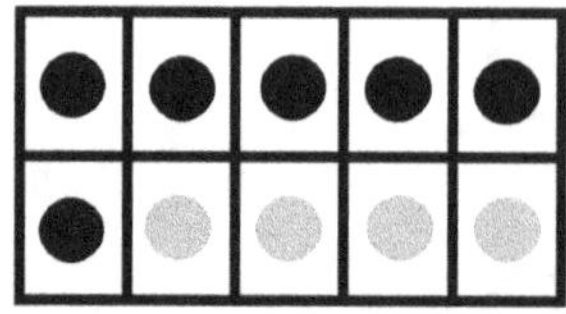

______ + ______ = ______

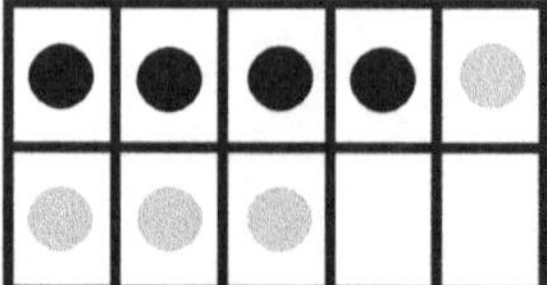

______ + ______ = ______

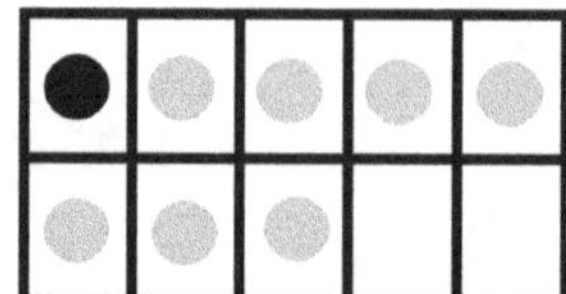

______ + ______ = ______

Addition Practice—Sums to 10

Write the number sentence.

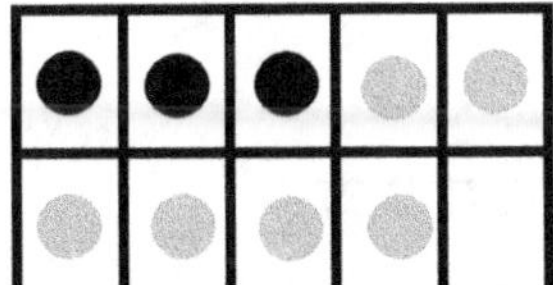

______ + ______ = ______

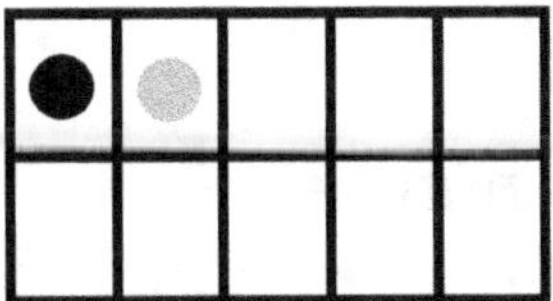

______ + ______ = ______

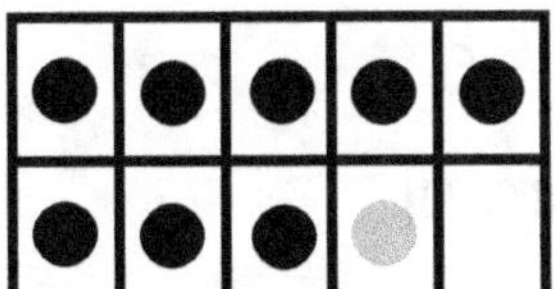

______ + ______ = ______

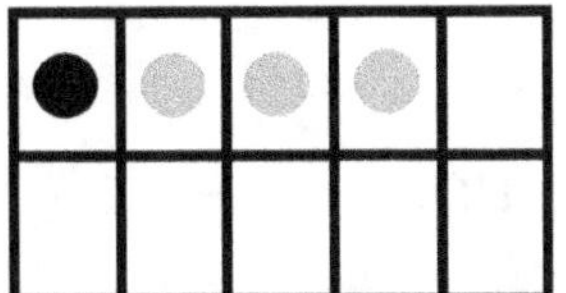

______ + ______ = ______

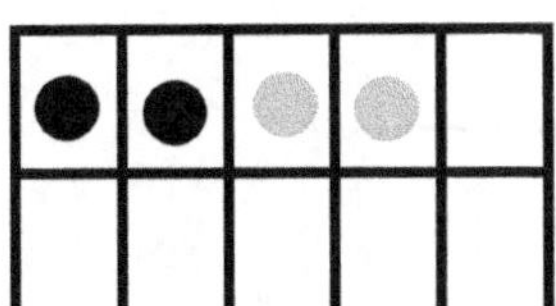

______ + ______ = ______

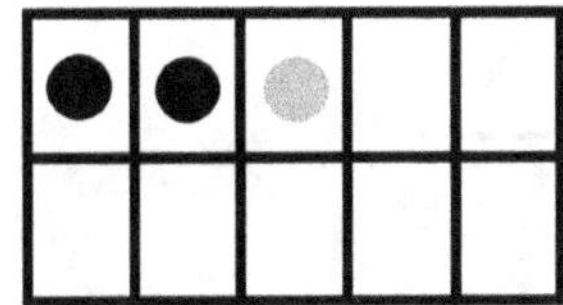

______ + ______ = ______

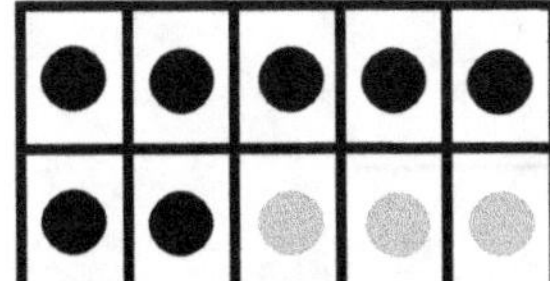

______ + ______ = ______

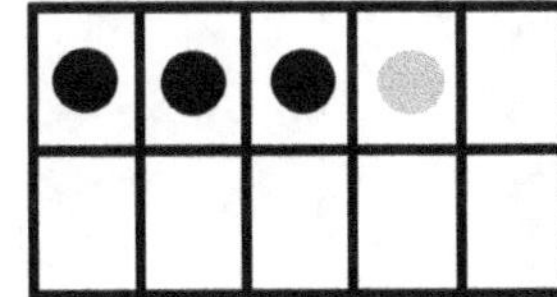

______ + ______ = ______

______ + ______ = ______

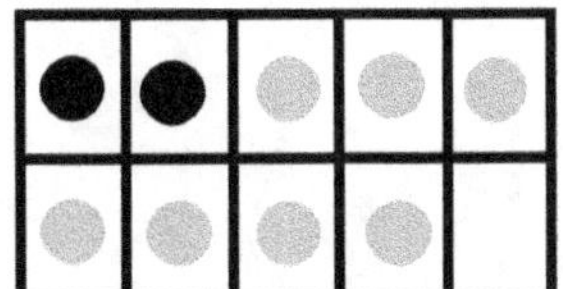

______ + ______ = ______

Add 1 or 2 by Counting On

<table>
<tr><td>

Add 1 by counting on.

4 + 1 = _____

Start with the greater number.

Count on by 1.

   4   5

Stop when 1 finger is up.

4 + 1 = __5__

</td><td>

Add 2 by counting on.

4 + 2 = _____

Start with the greater number.

Count on by 2.

   4   5   6

Stop when 2 fingers are up.

4 + 2 = __6__

</td></tr>
</table>

Count on to add.

6 + 1 = _____ 6, ____	5 + 2 = _____ 5, ____, ____
2 + 1 = _____ 2, ____	3 + 2 = _____ 3, ____, ____
8 + 1 = _____ 8, ____	1 + 2 = _____ 1, ____, ____
3 + 1 = _____ 3, ____	7 + 2 = _____ 7, ____, ____

Add 1 or 2 by Counting On

Count on to add.

4 + 1 = _____ 4, _____	2 + 2 = _____ 2, _____, _____
9 + 1 = _____ 9, _____	4 + 2 = _____ 4, _____, _____
7 + 1 = _____ 7, _____	8 + 2 = _____ 8, _____, _____
1 + 1 = _____ 1, _____	6 + 2 = _____ 6, _____, _____
5 + 1 = _____ 5, _____	0 + 2 = _____ 0, _____, _____
0 + 1 = _____ 0, _____	9 + 2 = _____ 9, _____, _____

Use a Number Line to Add

Use a number line to add.

6 + 3 = __9__

Mark a dot at 6.
Draw 3 jumps to count on.
Stop at 9.

Use the number line to add. Mark a dot to show where to start.
Next, count on by drawing the jumps. Write the answer.

3 + 6 = ____

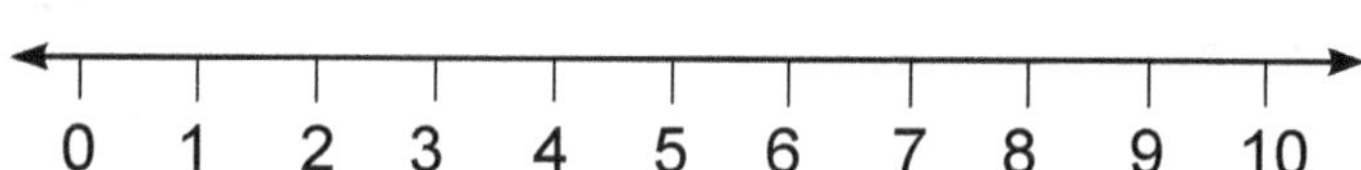

4 + 4 = ____

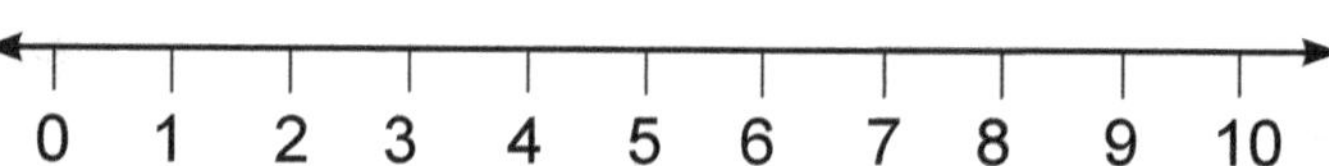

0 + 8 = ____

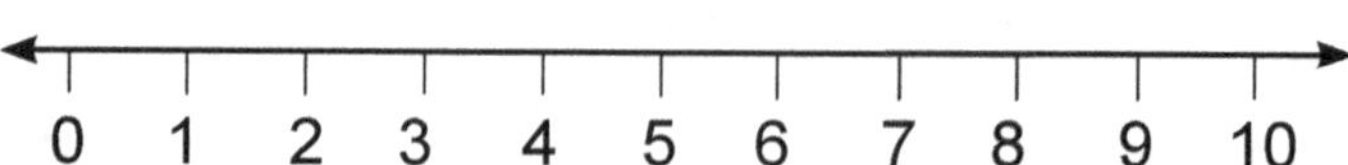

1 + 7 = ____

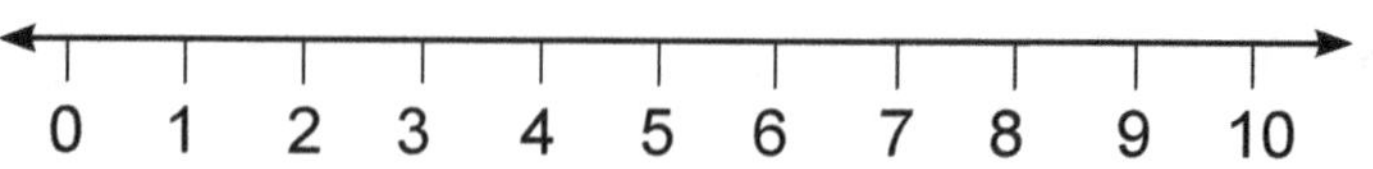

5 + 4 = ____

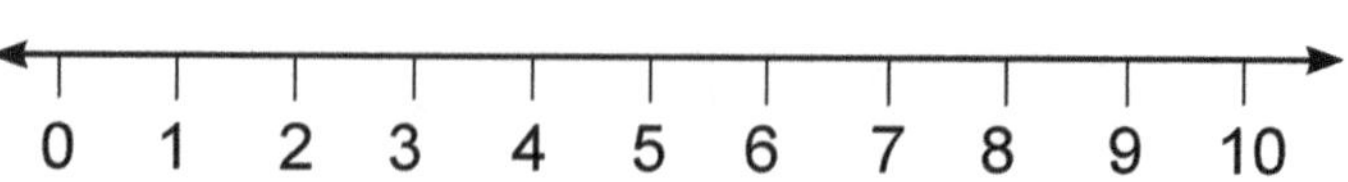

Use a Number Line to Add

Use the number line to add by counting on. Mark a dot to show where to start. Next, draw the jumps. Write the answer.

0 + 7 = _____ 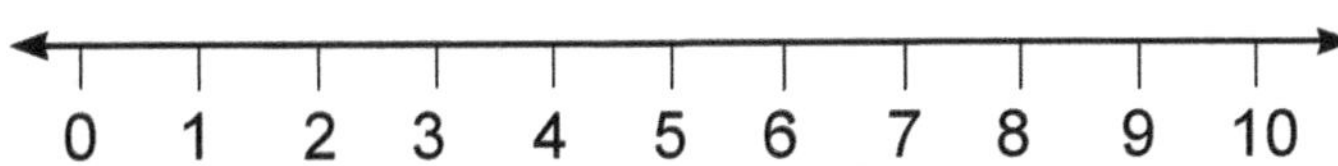

8 + 2 = _____ 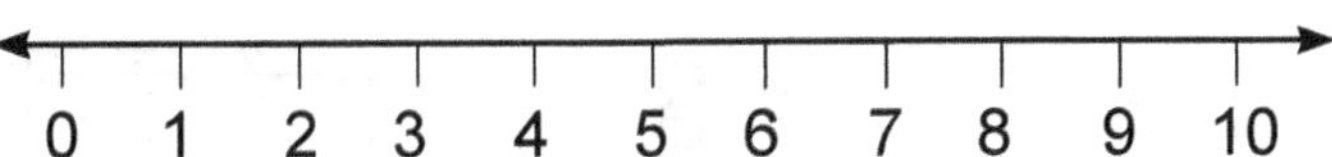

9 + 1 = _____ 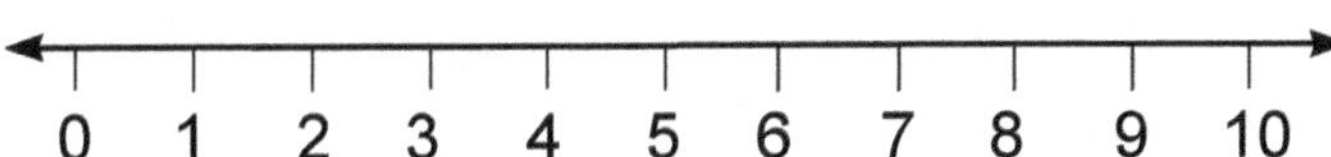

2 + 6 = _____ 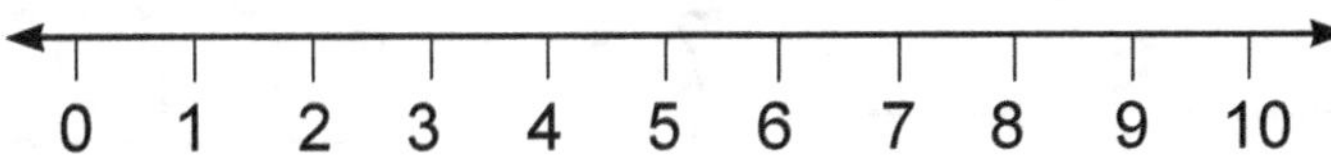

4 + 3 = _____ 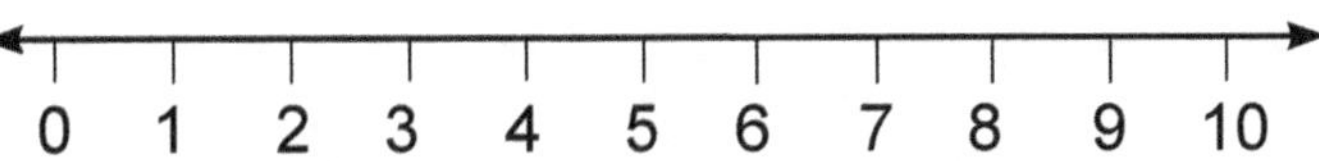

1 + 8 = _____ 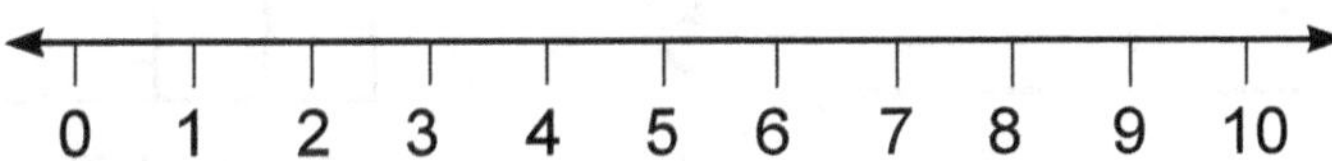

3 + 3 = _____ 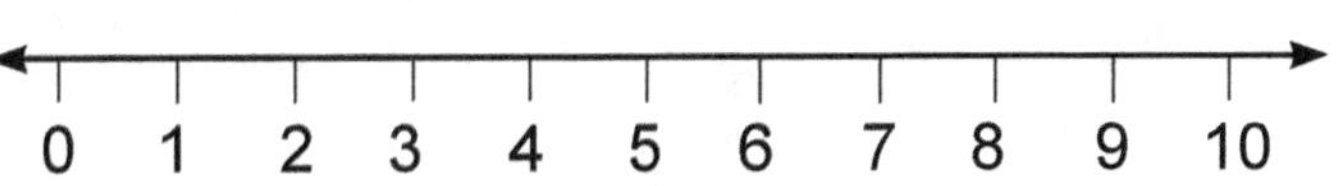

2 + 4 = _____

Make Addition Sentences

Show three ways to make each number. Use two colors to color the blocks.

___ + ___ = 9

___ + ___ = 9

___ + ___ = 9

___ + ___ = 3

___ + ___ = 3

___ + ___ = 3

___ + ___ = 7

___ + ___ = 7

___ + ___ = 7

___ + ___ = 5

___ + ___ = 5

___ + ___ = 5

Make Addition Sentences

Show three ways to make each number. Use two colors to color the blocks.

___ + ___ = 10 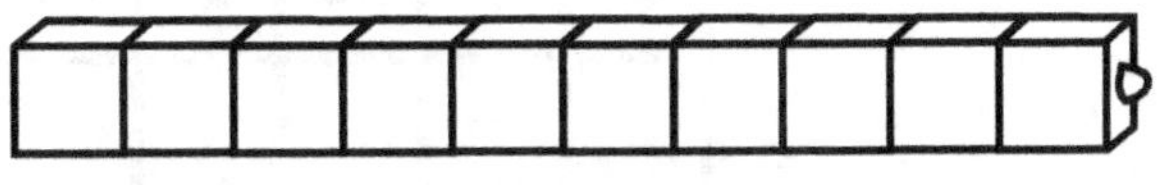

___ + ___ = 10

___ + ___ = 10

___ + ___ = 8 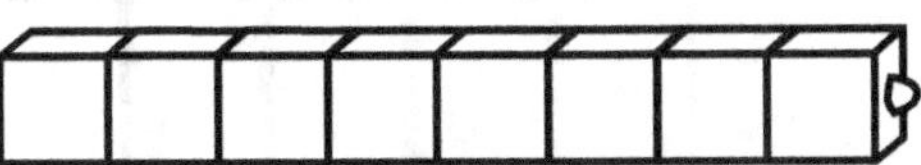

___ + ___ = 8

___ + ___ = 8

___ + ___ = 6 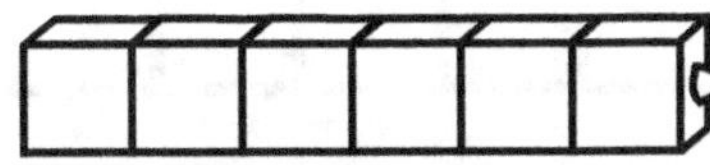

___ + ___ = 6

___ + ___ = 6

___ + ___ = 4 

___ + ___ = 4

___ + ___ = 4

Numbers Can Be Added in Any Order

5 + 2 = 7

2 + 5 = 7

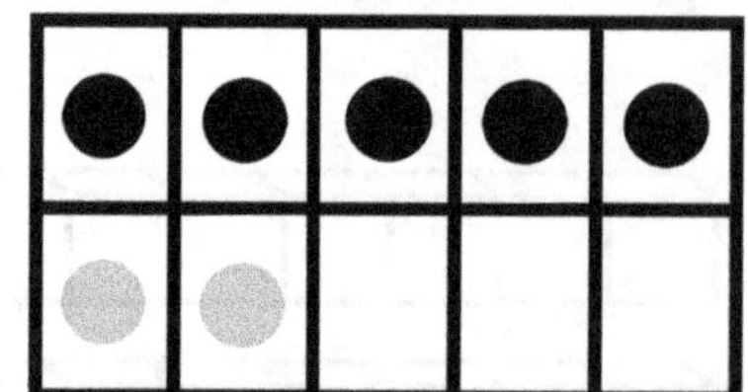

Use the ten frames to show adding numbers in two ways.
Use two different colors. Then, write the answers.

6 + 2 = _____

2 + 6 = _____

=

3 + 4 = _____

4 + 3 = _____

=

1 + 8 = _____

8 + 1 = _____

=

4 + 5 = _____

5 + 4 = _____

=

7 + 2 = _____

2 + 7 = _____

=

© Chalkboard Publishing

Numbers Can Be Added in Any Order

Use the ten frames to show adding numbers in two ways.
Use two different colors. Then, write the answers.

6 + 4 = _____
4 + 6 = _____

2 + 3 = _____
3 + 2 = _____

1 + 7 = _____
7 + 1 = _____

5 + 3 = _____
3 + 5 = _____

1 + 3 = _____
3 + 1 = _____

Make your own number sentence. Use numbers that are less than 10.

_____ + _____ = _____ + _____ 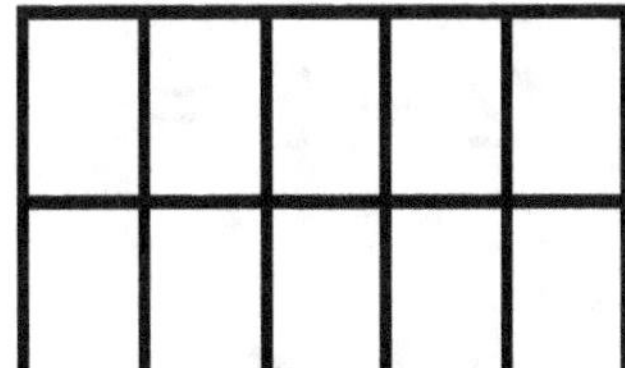 = 

Addition Practice—Sums to 10

Use the key to color the picture.

Color Key
- 1 – red
- 2 – yellow
- 3 – purple
- 5 – gray
- 7 – orange
- 9 – blue
- 10 – black

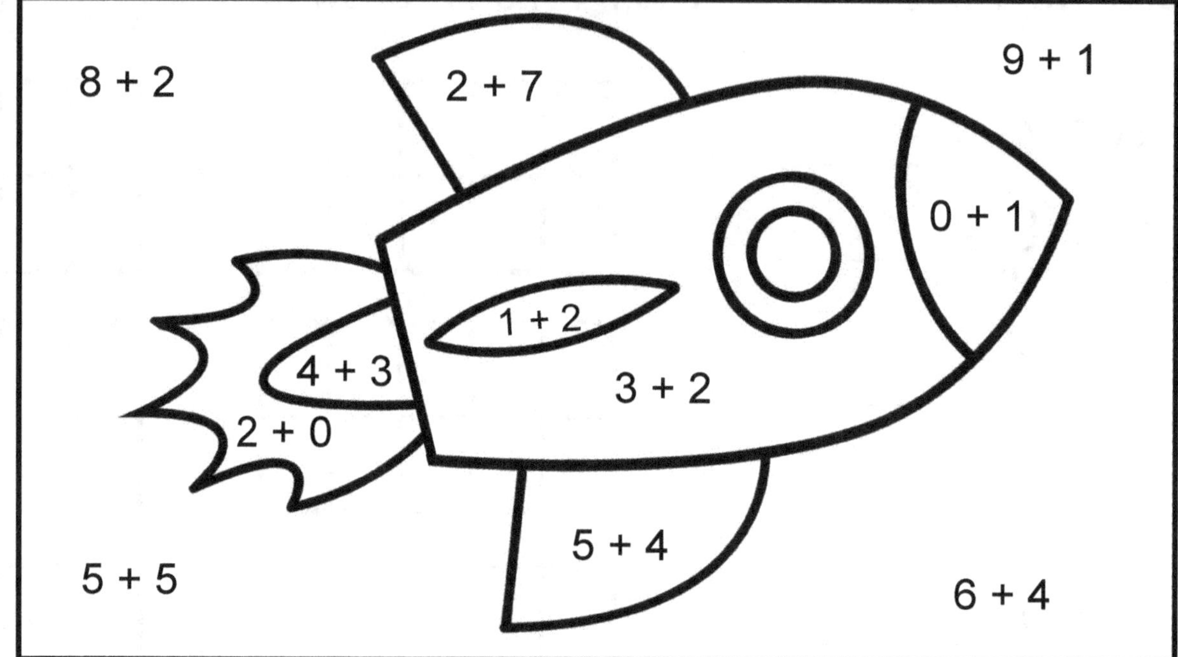

Complete the sums.

2 + 1 = _____	8 + 1 = _____	3 + 6 = _____
5 + 2 = _____	6 + 0 = _____	0 + 3 = _____
3 + 4 = _____	1 + 1 = _____	1 + 0 = _____
2 + 2 = _____	1 + 5 = _____	4 + 4 = _____
3 + 1 = _____	2 + 3 = _____	4 + 1 = _____
2 + 5 = _____	6 + 1 = _____	3 + 7 = _____

Addition Facts to 10

Match the number sentence to the correct answer.

4 + 4 =	7	2 + 3
0 + 1 =	**8**	6 + 3
1 + 3 =	6	1 + 1
2 + 4 =	5	3 + 0
3 + 7 =	9	5 + 5
1 + 2 =	2	1 + 0
8 + 1 =	4	4 + 3
2 + 5 =	10	3 + 3
0 + 2 =	1	5 + 3
1 + 4 =	3	2 + 2

BRAIN STRETCH

4 + 1 + 5 =   7 + 2 + 1 =

Math Riddle: Addition Facts to 10

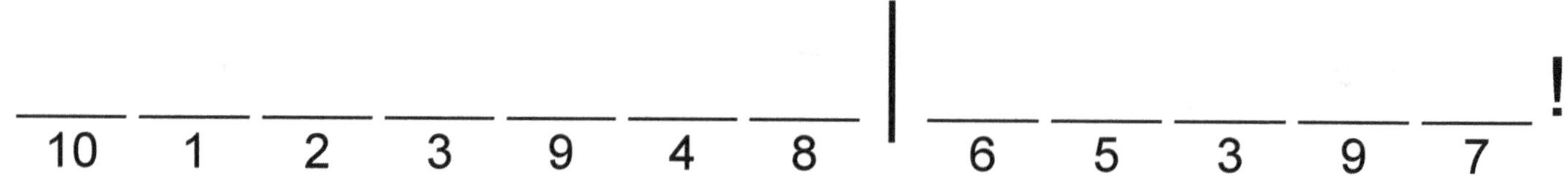

___ ___ ___ ___ ___ ___ | ___ ___ ___ ___ ___ !
10 1 2 3 9 4 8   6 5 3 9 7

A	C	E
5 + 4	2 + 4	2 + 1
K 1 + 3	**L** 3 + 2	**N** 2 + 5
Q 1 + 0	**S** 6 + 4	**U** 1 + 1
Y 3 + 5		

Add.

6 + 4	1 + 1	5 + 2	3 + 6	2 + 7
0 + 1	5 + 0	2 + 3	1 + 2	0 + 7
3 + 4	4 + 4	3 + 3	7 + 3	3 + 5
2 + 5	6 + 1	8 + 2	2 + 2	4 + 5

BRAIN STRETCH

$1 + 4 + 5 =$ $2 + 3 + 5 =$

Addition Doubles

Write the number sentence.

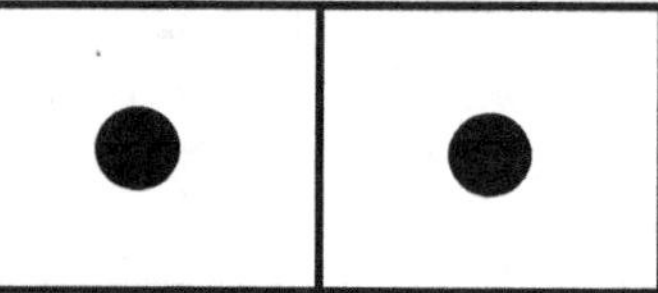

_____ + _____ = _____

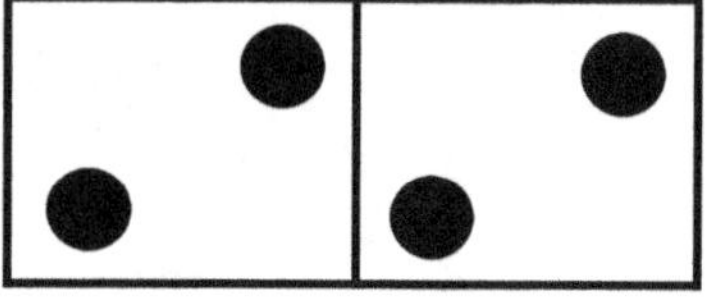

_____ + _____ = _____

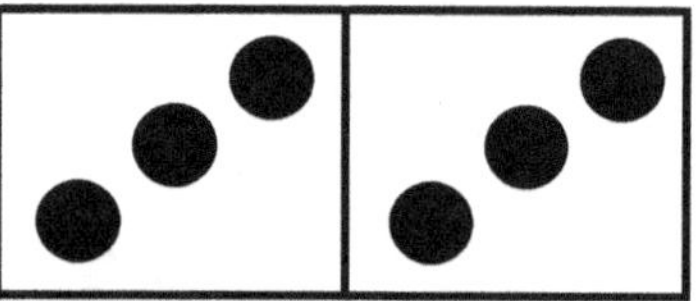

_____ + _____ = _____

_____ + _____ = _____

_____ + _____ = _____

_____ + _____ = _____

Addition Doubles Plus 1

Use doubles plus 1 to add.

If $\quad 6 + 6 = \underline{\textbf{12}}$	If $\quad 10 + 10 = \underline{}$
Then $\; 6 + 7 = \underline{\textbf{13}}$	Then $\underline{} + \underline{} = \underline{}$
If $\quad 3 + 3 = \underline{}$	If $\quad 5 + 5 = \underline{}$
Then $\underline{} + \underline{} = \underline{}$	Then $\underline{} + \underline{} = \underline{}$
If $\quad 8 + 8 = \underline{}$	If $\quad 1 + 1 = \underline{}$
Then $\underline{} + \underline{} = \underline{}$	Then $\underline{} + \underline{} = \underline{}$
If $\quad 9 + 9 = \underline{}$	If $\quad 2 + 2 = \underline{}$
Then $\underline{} + \underline{} = \underline{}$	Then $\underline{} + \underline{} = \underline{}$
If $\quad 4 + 4 = \underline{}$	If $\quad 7 + 7 = \underline{}$
Then $\underline{} + \underline{} = \underline{}$	Then $\underline{} + \underline{} = \underline{}$

Add by Making 10

Make a group of 10 to help you add.

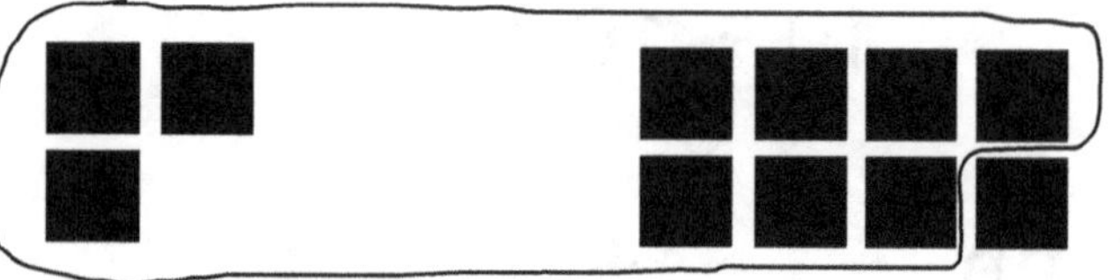

$3 + 8 = 10 + \underline{1} = \underline{11}$

Circle 10. There is 1 more block. Use 10 to add.

$5 + 8 = 10 + \underline{} = \underline{}$

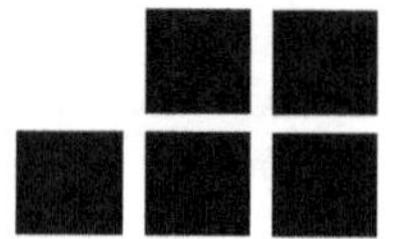 

$5 + 7 = 10 + \underline{} = \underline{}$

$7 + 7 = 10 + \underline{} = \underline{}$

$4 + 9 = 10 + \underline{} = \underline{}$

$9 + 6 = 10 + \underline{} = \underline{}$

Add by Making 10

Make a group of 10 to help you add.

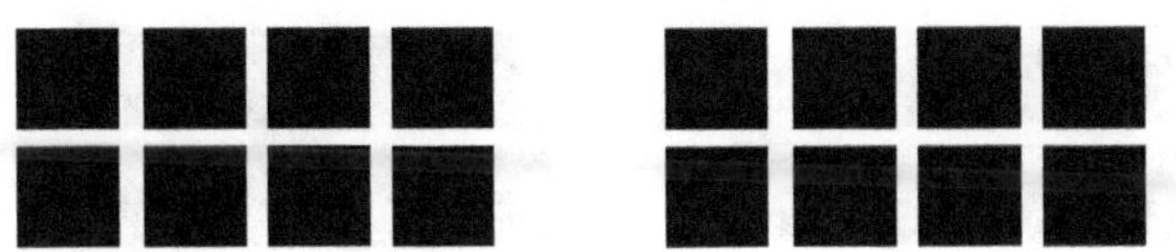

8 + 8 = 10 + ___ = ___

6 + 5 = 10 + ___ = ___

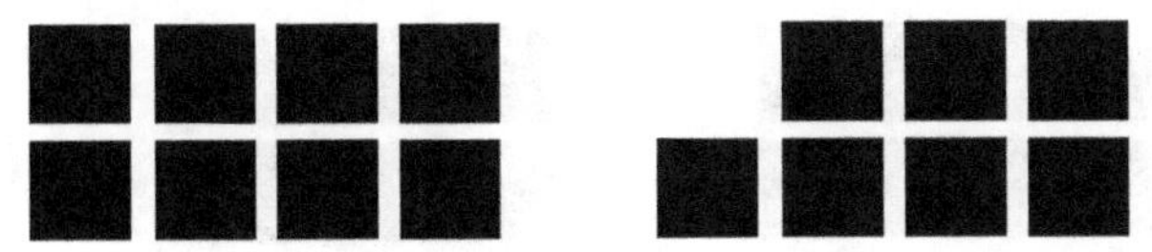

8 + 7 = 10 + ___ = ___

5 + 9 = 10 + ___ = ___

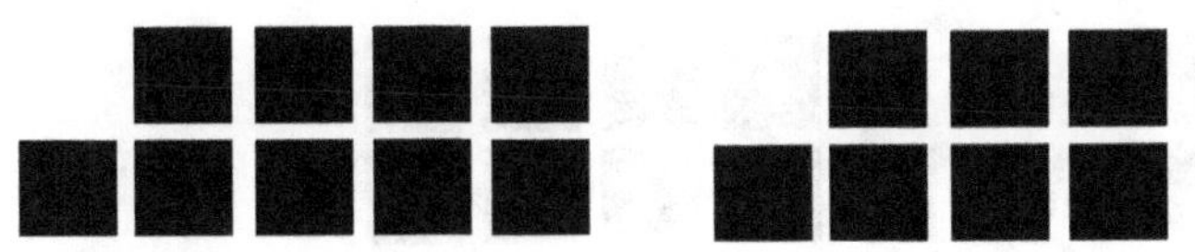

9 + 7 = 10 + ___ = ___

9 + 9 = 10 + ___ = ___

Add by Making 10

Make a group of 10 to help you add.

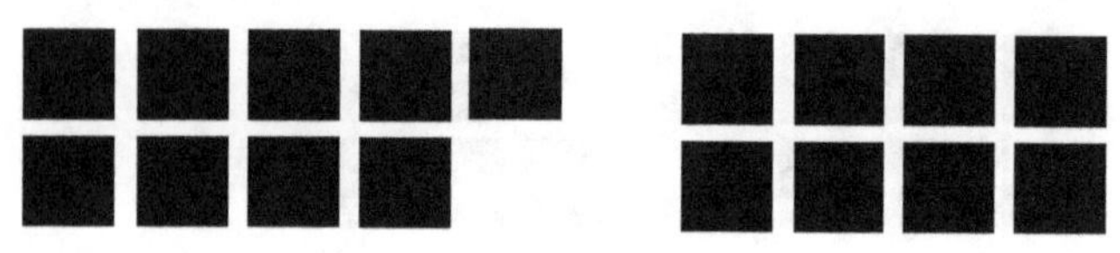

$9 + 8 = 10 + \underline{} = \underline{}$

$7 + 8 = 10 + \underline{} = \underline{}$

$6 + 9 = 10 + \underline{} = \underline{}$

$8 + 6 = 10 + \underline{} = \underline{}$

$9 + 4 = 10 + \underline{} = \underline{}$

$2 + 9 = 10 + \underline{} = \underline{}$

Take Apart to Make 10

9 + 5 = 14

9 + 5 = 10 + 4 = 14
I know 9 + 1 = 10, so I broke 5 into 1 and 4.
Then I have to add 4 more. The sum is 14.

Make 10 to add.

8 + 6 = 10 + ___ = ___

Draw a model. Make 10 to add.

5 + 8 = 10 + ___ = ___

4 + 7 = 10 + ___ = ___

9 + 9 = 10 + ___ = ___

Draw a model. Make 10 to add.

6 + 6 = 10 + ___ = ___

5 + 9 = 10 + ___ = ___

7 + 8 = 10 + ___ = ___

8 + 8 = 10 + ___ = ___

7 + 7 = 10 + ___ = ___

Draw a model. Make 10 to add.

8 + 7 = 10 + ___ = ___

4 + 9 = 10 + ___ = ___

9 + 6 = 10 + ___ = ___

5 + 7 = 10 + ___ = ___

3 + 9 = 10 + ___ = ___

Addition Practice—Sums from 11 to 20

Add. Use the number line or counters to help you.
Hint: Start with the greater number.

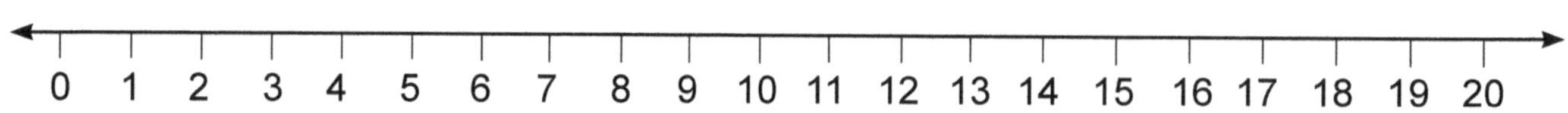

8	9	10	1	14
+ 6	+ 8	+ 5	+ 10	+ 3

5	15	11	8	7
+ 12	+ 5	+ 3	+ 8	+ 7

10	6	13	16	7
+ 10	+ 10	+ 1	+ 4	+ 5

9	5	9	8	10
+ 5	+ 7	+ 9	+ 5	+ 6

Add. Use the number line or counters to help you.
Hint: Start with the greater number.

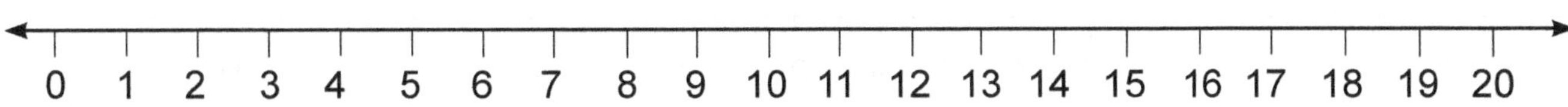

$\begin{array}{r} 7 \\ +\ 8 \\ \hline \end{array}$	$\begin{array}{r} 5 \\ +\ 5 \\ \hline \end{array}$	$\begin{array}{r} 12 \\ +\ 3 \\ \hline \end{array}$	$\begin{array}{r} 6 \\ +\ 6 \\ \hline \end{array}$	$\begin{array}{r} 15 \\ +\ 3 \\ \hline \end{array}$
$\begin{array}{r} 17 \\ +\ 2 \\ \hline \end{array}$	$\begin{array}{r} 11 \\ +\ 0 \\ \hline \end{array}$	$\begin{array}{r} 10 \\ +\ 3 \\ \hline \end{array}$	$\begin{array}{r} 9 \\ +\ 2 \\ \hline \end{array}$	$\begin{array}{r} 4 \\ +\ 9 \\ \hline \end{array}$
$\begin{array}{r} 8 \\ +\ 10 \\ \hline \end{array}$	$\begin{array}{r} 9 \\ +\ 7 \\ \hline \end{array}$	$\begin{array}{r} 7 \\ +\ 6 \\ \hline \end{array}$	$\begin{array}{r} 18 \\ +\ 2 \\ \hline \end{array}$	$\begin{array}{r} 14 \\ +\ 3 \\ \hline \end{array}$
$\begin{array}{r} 5 \\ +\ 9 \\ \hline \end{array}$	$\begin{array}{r} 11 \\ +\ 7 \\ \hline \end{array}$	$\begin{array}{r} 7 \\ +\ 4 \\ \hline \end{array}$	$\begin{array}{r} 5 \\ +\ 13 \\ \hline \end{array}$	$\begin{array}{r} 3 \\ +\ 12 \\ \hline \end{array}$

Missing Numbers

Fill in the missing number. Use the number line to help you.

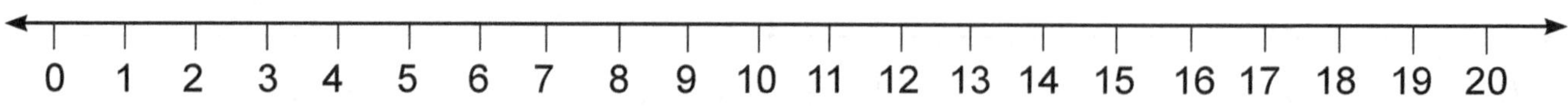

3 + ☐ 6	9 + ☐ 18	3 + ☐ 12	☐ + 6 14	4 + ☐ 15
9 + ☐ 17	☐ + 2 11	7 + ☐ 12	☐ + 7 13	10 + ☐ 19
3 + ☐ 5	7 + ☐ 7	☐ + 10 18	☐ + 9 14	1 + ☐ 11
☐ + 8 16	10 + ☐ 20	☐ + 4 10	2 + ☐ 6	10 + ☐ 15

Missing Numbers

Fill in the missing number. Use the number line to help you.

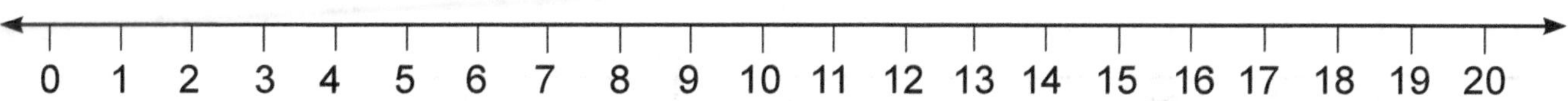

$$2 + \boxed{} = 7$$
$$17 + \boxed{} = 19$$
$$13 + \boxed{} = 14$$
$$\boxed{} + 6 = 10$$
$$3 + \boxed{} = 11$$

$$10 + \boxed{} = 20$$
$$\boxed{} + 1 = 17$$
$$\boxed{} + 7 = 9$$
$$\boxed{} + 6 = 11$$
$$5 + \boxed{} = 10$$

$$3 + \boxed{} = 8$$
$$5 + \boxed{} = 9$$
$$\boxed{} + 11 = 16$$
$$\boxed{} + 6 = 12$$
$$1 + \boxed{} = 15$$

$$\boxed{} + 8 = 10$$
$$5 + \boxed{} = 20$$
$$\boxed{} + 4 = 7$$
$$2 + \boxed{} = 12$$
$$10 + \boxed{} = 16$$

Why did the turkey cross the road?

___ ___ | ___ ___ ___ ___ ___ | ___ ___ |
8 9 | 10 20 9 15 16 | 17 16 |

___ ___ ___ ___ ___ , ___ | ___ ___ ___ ___ ___ ___ ___ !
7 19 11 14 8 | 13 17 12 13 18 16 14

A	C	D	E	H
10 + 9	7 + 6	2 + 1	9 + 7	10 + 7

I	K	L	N	O
8 + 4	9 + 9	3 + 3	8 + 6	5 + 4

P	R	S	T	U
8 + 2	10 +10	9 + 2	7 + 1	3 + 2

V	W	Y
9 + 6	4 + 3	2 + 2

Watch out! Some letters are not used in the riddle.

Use a Number Line to Add

You can find the sum of two numbers by counting on.

14 + 5 = 19   Count: 14, 15, 16, 17, 18, 19

Use the number line to find the sum.

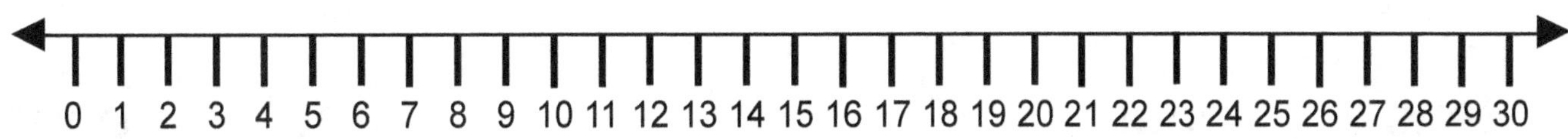

24 + 4 =

15 + 3 =

24 + 5 =

16 + 9 =

5 + 12 =

21 + 5 =

18 + 5 =

15 + 7 =

Practice Regrouping Ones as Tens

Count and regroup ones as tens.

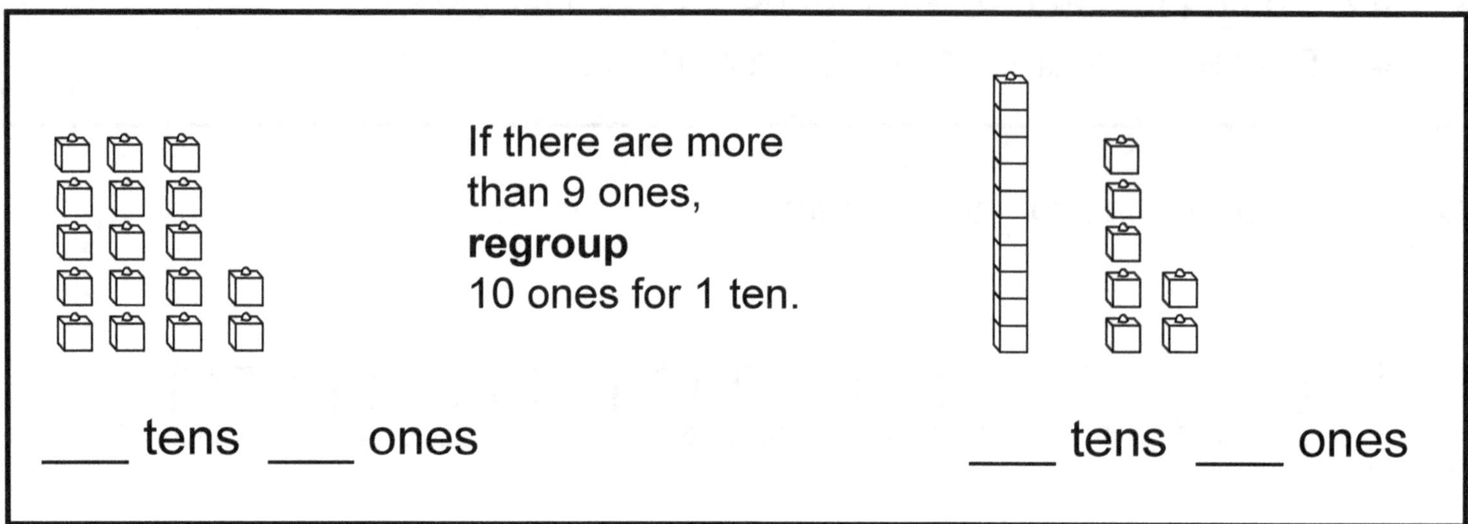

If there are more than 9 ones, **regroup** 10 ones for 1 ten.

___ tens ___ ones ___ tens ___ ones

regroup

___ tens ___ ones ___ tens ___ ones

regroup

___ tens ___ ones ___ tens ___ ones

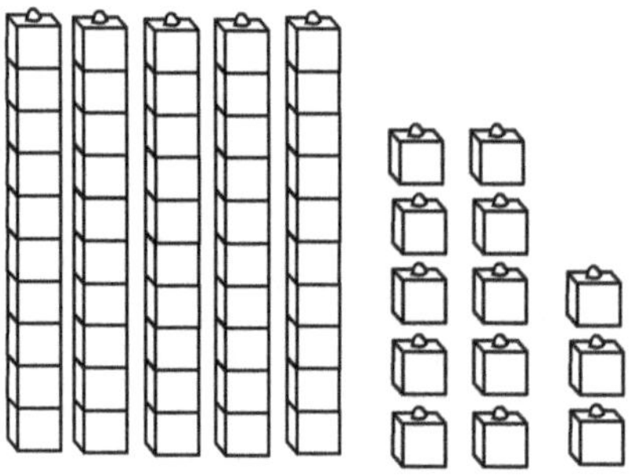

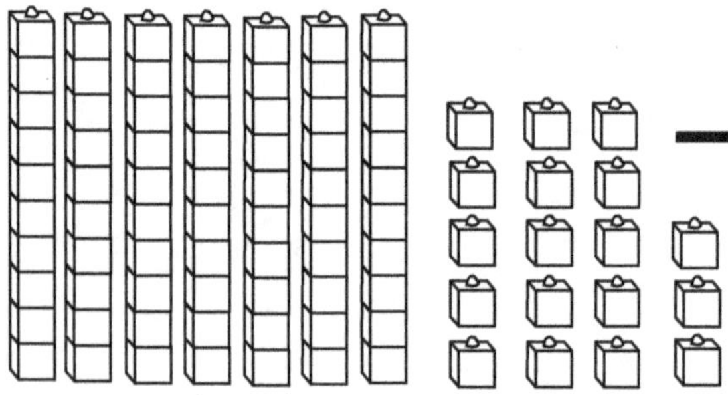

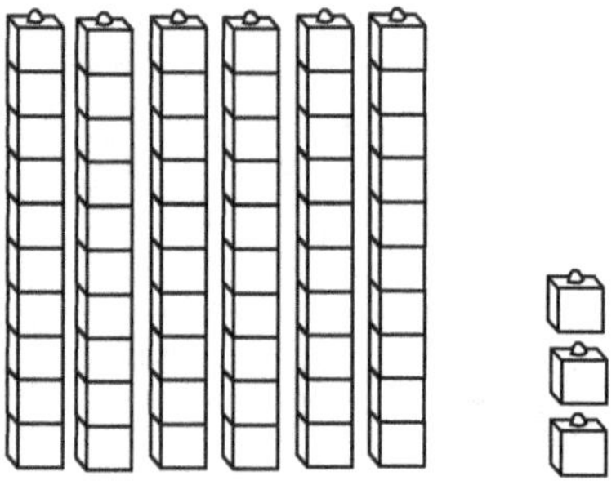

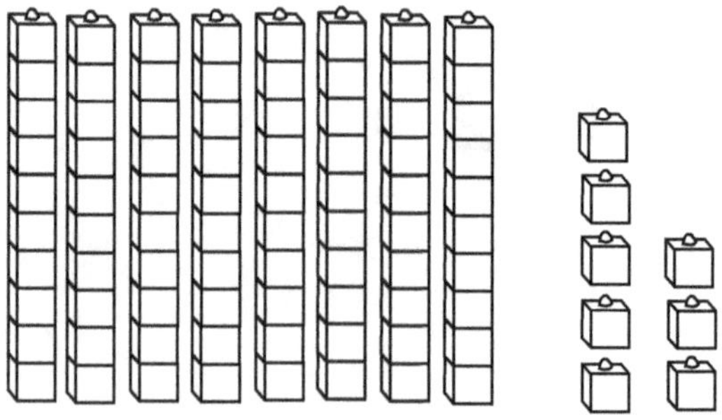

Practice Regrouping Ones as Tens

Count and regroup ones as tens.

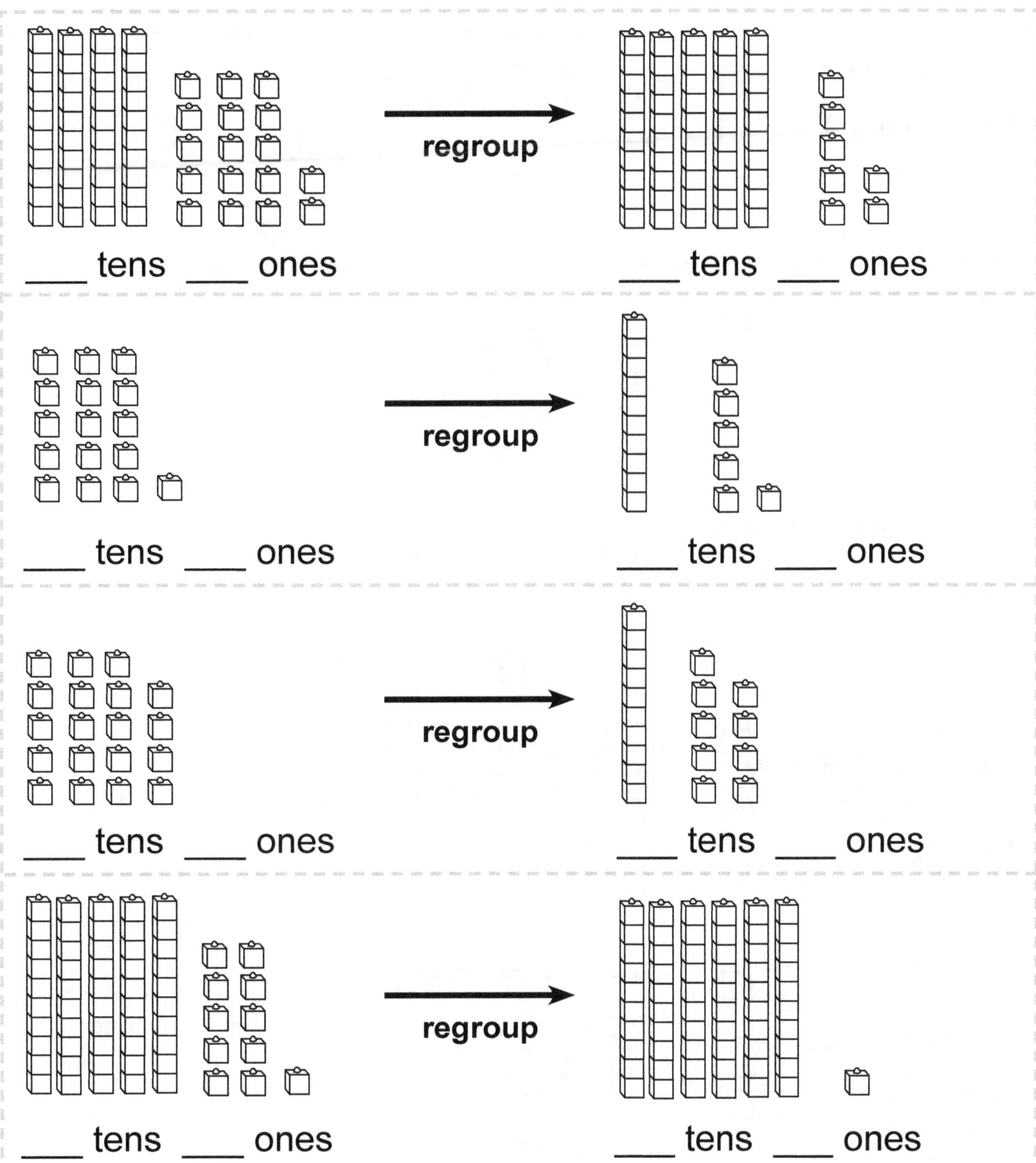

___ tens ___ ones → regroup → ___ tens ___ ones

___ tens ___ ones → regroup → ___ tens ___ ones

___ tens ___ ones → regroup → ___ tens ___ ones

___ tens ___ ones → regroup → ___ tens ___ ones

Adding Tens and Ones

Use tens and ones to add.

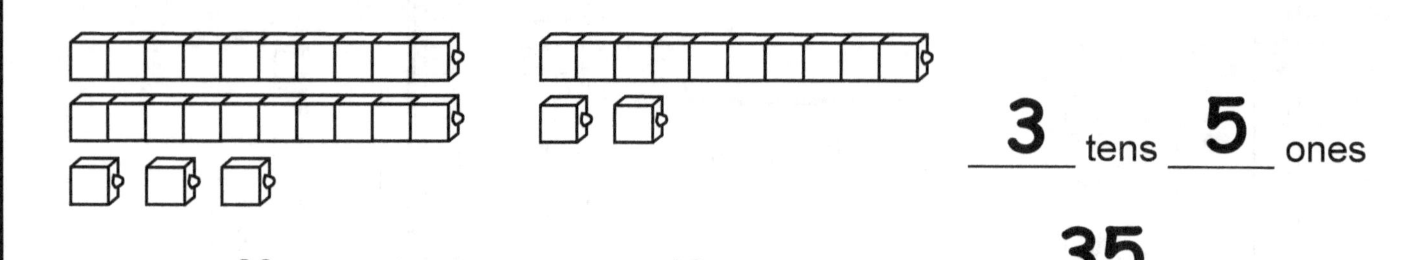

3 tens 5 ones

35

23 + 12 =

_____ tens _____ ones

14 + 25 = _______

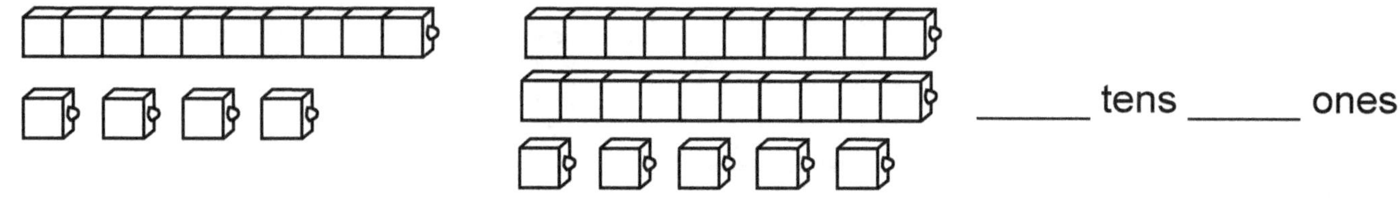

_____ tens _____ ones

11 + 12 = _______

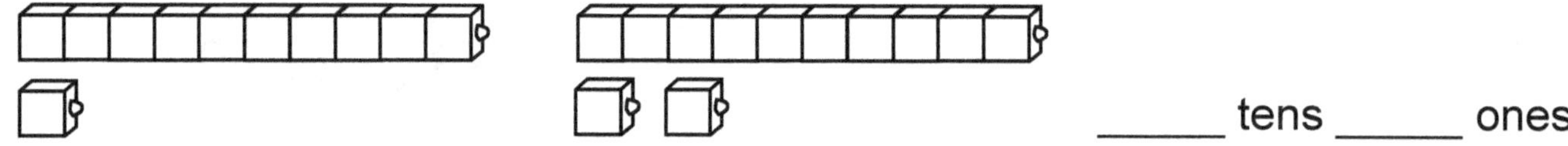

_____ tens _____ ones

32 + 17 = _______

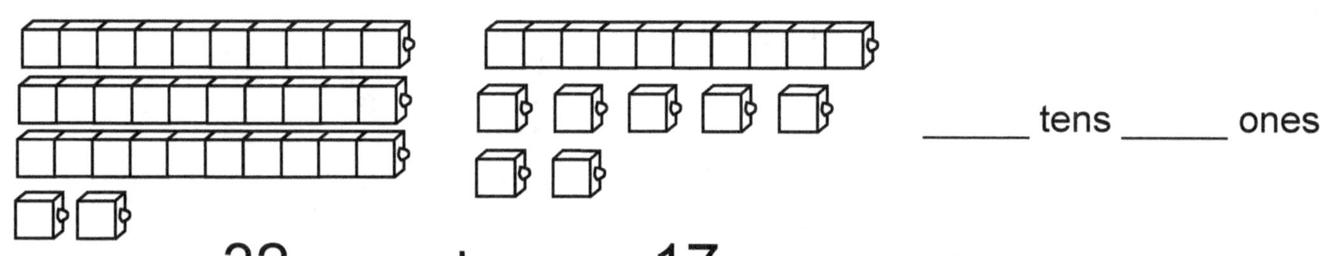

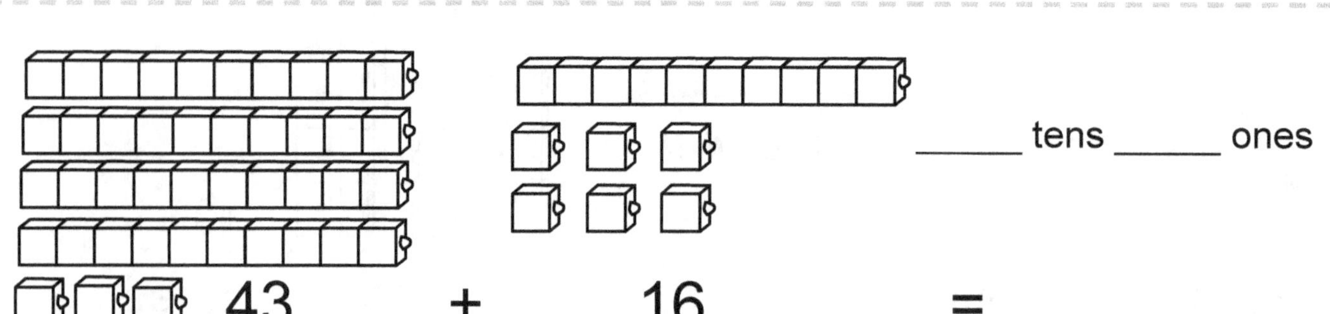

_____ tens _____ ones

43 + 16 = _______

© Chalkboard Publishing

Use tens and ones to add.

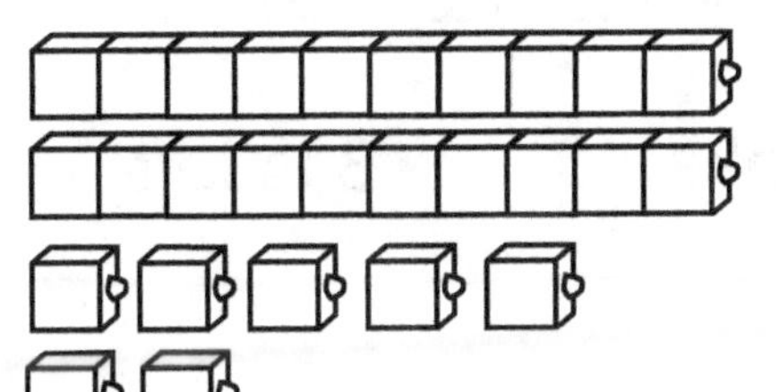 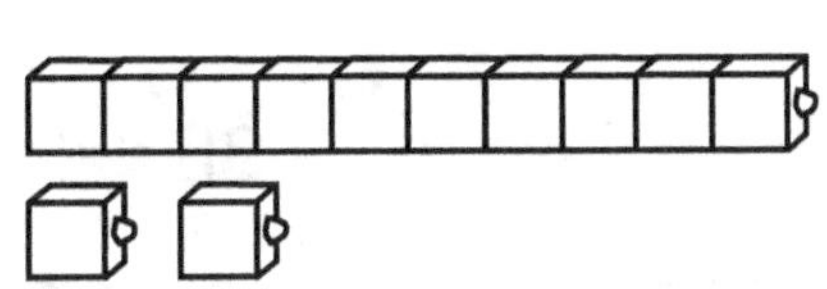

_____ tens _____ ones

27 + 12 = _______

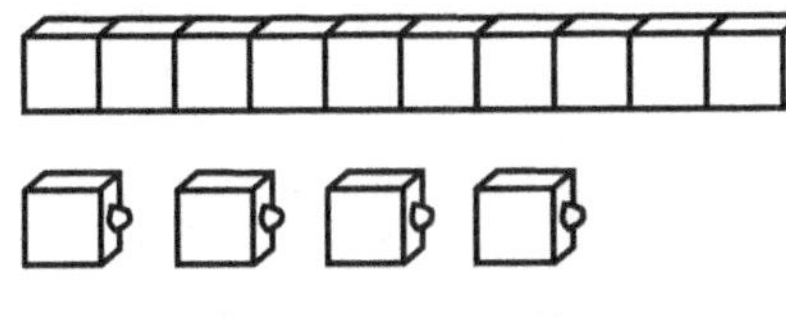 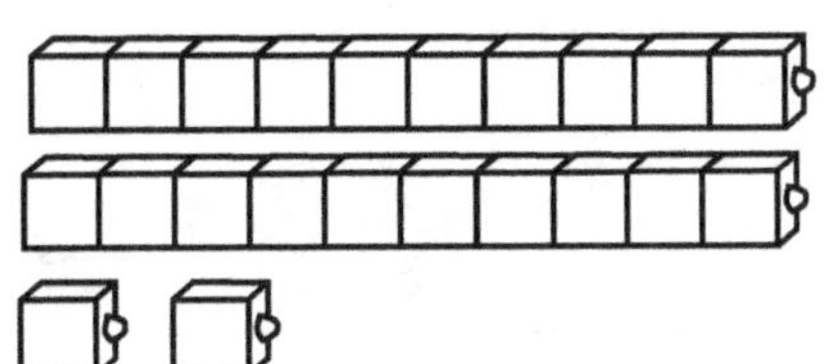

_____ tens _____ ones

14 + 22 = _______

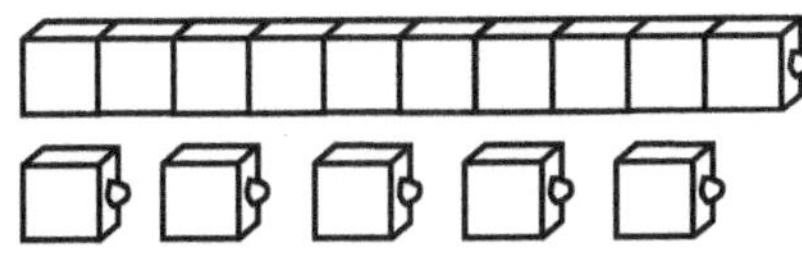 

_____ tens _____ ones

15 + 11 = _______

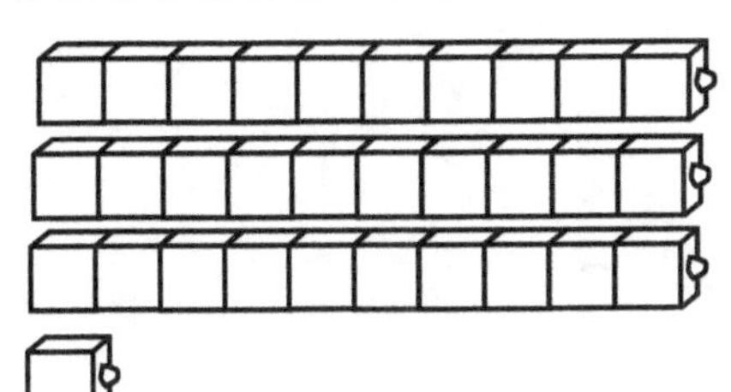

_____ tens _____ ones

31 + 10 = _______

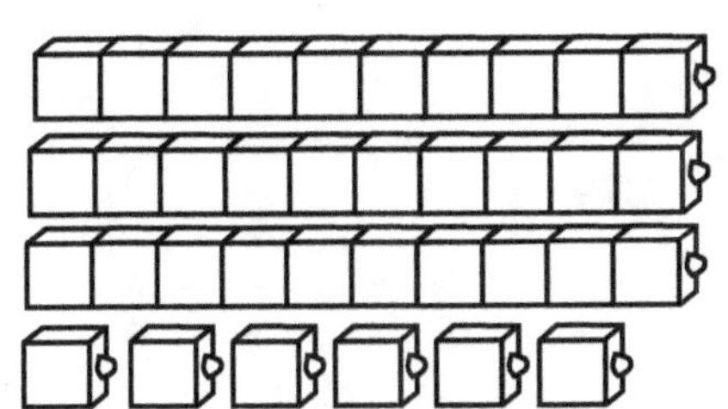 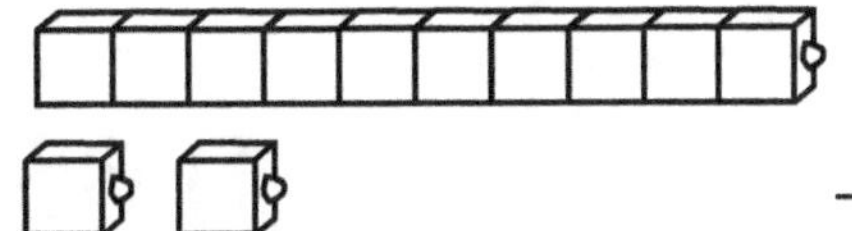

_____ tens _____ ones

36 + 12 = _______

Take Apart to Make Tens

$9 + 5 = (9 + \underline{1}) + (\underline{4}) = \underline{10} + \underline{4} = \underline{14}$

$9 + 1$ make 10   4 is left

$38 + 5 = (38 + \underline{2}) + (\underline{3}) = \underline{40} + \underline{3} = \underline{43}$

$38 + 2$ make 40   3 is left

Use tens to add.

a) $8 + 7 =$ ___ + ___ + ___ = ___ + ___ = ___

b) $25 + 9 =$ ___ + ___ + ___ = ___ + ___ = ___

Use tens to add. Show your work.

a) $34 + 7 =$

b) $49 + 4 =$

c) $73 + 8 =$

d) $59 + 5 =$

e) $48 + 8 =$

f) $65 + 7 =$

Take Apart to Make Tens

Use tens to add. Show your work.

a) 16 + 8 =

b) 37 + 9 =

c) 63 + 9 =

d) 37 + 8 =

e) 44 + 7 =

f) 55 + 7 =

g) 62 + 9 =

h) 77 + 7 =

i) 17 + 6 =

j) 53 + 9 =

Two-Digit Addition Without Regrouping

Line up the ones and tens.

First add the ones.

tens	ones
2	3
+ 4	5
	8

Then add the tens.

tens	ones
2	3
+ 4	5
6	8

Use a tens and ones chart to add. Shade the ones column yellow. Shade the tens column orange.

tens | ones

| 5 4 | 2 2 | 7 1 | 3 5 | 4 4 |
| + 3 1 | + 1 5 | + 2 7 | + 6 2 | + 3 0 |

| 1 2 | 7 6 | 6 2 | 8 4 | 3 3 |
| + 5 0 | + 1 2 | + 2 3 | + 1 1 | + 1 3 |

| 5 4 | 3 1 | 5 3 | 6 2 | 1 4 |
| + 3 3 | + 2 6 | + 1 1 | + 3 7 | + 3 0 |

| 8 2 | 1 2 | 3 4 | 2 0 | 5 2 |
| + 1 5 | + 4 0 | + 1 4 | + 1 3 | + 4 3 |

Two-Digit Addition Without Regrouping

Use a tens and ones chart to add. Shade the ones column yellow. Shade the tens column orange.

tens   ones

8	3
+ 1	4

1	3
+ 4	3

3	6
+ 1	3

2	1
+ 3	2

5	3
+ 4	6

5	5
+ 3	0

2	3
+ 2	5

7	2
+ 2	6

1	6
+ 6	0

4	5
+ 3	2

1	3
+ 5	0

7	7
+ 1	1

6	3
+ 1	3

8	5
+ 1	4

3	4
+ 1	5

5	1
+ 2	1

3	2
+ 2	2

5	4
+ 1	2

4	3
+ 3	6

1	5
+ 3	3

7	2
+ 2	5

2	4
+ 3	2

4	6
+ 1	2

1	1
+ 5	5

8	2
+ 1	6

Two-Digit Addition Without Regrouping

Use a tens and ones chart to add. Shade the ones column yellow.
Shade the tens column orange.

tens   ones

2 | 5	4 | 4	7 | 2	1 | 6	4 | 7
+ 1 | 4	+ 4 | 1	+ 1 | 7	+ 3 | 0	+ 5 | 0

| 3 \| 0 | 1 \| 2 | 5 \| 5 | 1 \| 2 | 3 \| 2 |
| + 3 \| 1 | + 4 \| 3 | + 3 \| 2 | + 5 \| 4 | + 4 \| 6 |

| 6 \| 3 | 2 \| 4 | 4 \| 5 | 7 \| 1 | 1 \| 2 |
| + 2 \| 4 | + 3 \| 4 | + 4 \| 3 | + 2 \| 2 | + 8 \| 3 |

| 1 \| 4 | 4 \| 6 | 1 \| 5 | 2 \| 1 | 7 \| 3 |
| + 7 \| 4 | + 5 \| 3 | + 4 \| 2 | + 6 \| 6 | + 1 \| 2 |

| 8 \| 3 | 1 \| 3 | 3 \| 5 | 2 \| 1 | 5 \| 3 |
| + 1 \| 2 | + 4 \| 5 | + 1 \| 3 | + 3 \| 8 | + 4 \| 5 |

Use a tens and ones chart to add. Shade the ones column yellow.
Shade the tens column orange.

| tens | ones |

```
  9|5        3|2        5|5        6|1        2|2
+  |3      + 3|6      + 1|4      + 2|3      +  |4
```

```
  4|8        3|3        2|1        2|2        4|2
+ 3|1      + 4|5      + 7|0      + 5|4      + 4|6
```

```
  1|7        8|2        3|7        5|0        4|5
+ 5|2      + 1|3      + 3|0      + 2|9      + 1|3
```

```
  7|6        5|5        3|3        2|1        7|0
+ 2|1      + 2|3      + 4|2      + 6|7      +  |5
```

```
  5|2        1|3        6|4        3|1        2|4
+ 4|7      + 2|3      + 3|4      + 1|1      + 2|5
```

Math Riddle: Two-Digit Addition Without Regrouping

Why are snakes hard to fool?

___ ___ ___ ___ | ___ ___ ___ ___ | ___ ___ |
33   52   61   54 | 52   65   57   61 | 79   63

___ ___ ___ ___ | ___ ___ | ___ ___ ___ ___ !
76   61   85   99 | 33   63 | 73   50   76   76

A	B	E	F	G	H
12 + 53	27 + 21	20 + 41	31 + 36	53 + 32	11 + 41
I	**L**	**M**	**N**	**O**	**P**
51 + 26	42 + 34	74 + 14	36 + 43	41 + 22	22 + 51
Q	**R**	**S**	**T**	**U**	**V**
20 + 60	77 + 20	56 + 43	12 + 21	20 + 30	12 + 45
Y	**Z**				
22 + 32	31 + 44				

Watch out! Some letters are not used in the riddle.

Two-Digit Addition with Regrouping

Line up the ones and the tens.
Add the ones.
If there are more than 9 ones, trade 10 ones for 1 ten.
Regroup in the tens column.
Write the ones. Then write the tens.

	tens	ones
	1	
	2	6
+	2	6
	5	2

Trade 10 ones from 12 for 1 ten.
Regroup by writing 1 in the tens column.

Use a tens and ones chart to add. Shade the ones column yellow.
Shade the tens column orange.

tens   ones

```
  6|4        2|2        4|5        3|9        4|9
+ 1|8      + 1|9      + 2|7      + 2|2      + 3|8
___________________________________________________


  1|2        7|6        6|4        2|9        3|6
+ 5|8      + 1|4      + 1|7      + 3|3      + 3|6
___________________________________________________


  5|4        3|5        2|5        6|2        1|7
+ 1|7      + 2|6      + 2|5      + 1|8      + 2|7
___________________________________________________
```

Use a tens and ones chart to add. Shade the ones column yellow.
Shade the tens column orange.

tens ones

| 1 | 7 | | 7 | 8 | | 6 | 4 | | 5 | 7 | | 3 | 5 |
| + 5 | 5 | | + 1 | 9 | | + 1 | 6 | | + 1 | 4 | | + 1 | 9 |

| 5 | 6 | | 2 | 4 | | 4 | 3 | | 2 | 7 | | 4 | 8 |
| + 3 | 8 | | + 2 | 6 | | + 2 | 9 | | + 6 | 6 | | + 3 | 8 |

| 4 | 7 | | 1 | 7 | | 3 | 4 | | 3 | 9 | | 5 | 5 |
| + 1 | 9 | | + 4 | 8 | | + 1 | 9 | | + 3 | 1 | | + 2 | 6 |

| 5 | 9 | | 3 | 9 | | 5 | 7 | | 6 | 4 | | 1 | 6 |
| + 2 | 3 | | + 2 | 8 | | + 1 | 6 | | + 2 | 7 | | + 3 | 8 |

| 7 | 4 | | 5 | 7 | | 6 | 2 | | 1 | 9 | | 2 | 9 |
| + 1 | 8 | | + 2 | 9 | | + 2 | 8 | | + 3 | 9 | | + 3 | 6 |

Two-Digit Addition with Regrouping

Use a tens and ones chart to add. Shade the ones column yellow.
Shade the tens column orange.

tens   ones

5|8	4|4	2|2	3|6	4|7
+ 2|4	+ 3|9	+ 3|8	+ 4|7	+ 3|9

3|9	1|2	5|5	1|8	3|8
+ 3|4	+ 4|9	+ 3|8	+ 5|4	+ 3|8

6|3	2|7	4|5	6|5	1|9
+ 2|8	+ 1|4	+ 4|6	+ 2|7	+ 1|9

1|9	4|6	2|9	2|6	7|6
+ 7|8	+ 3|8	+ 4|5	+ 6|6	+ 1|7

1|8	1|7	3|5	2|7	2|8
+ 1|4	+ 4|3	+ 1|9	+ 2|7	+ 4|5

Two-Digit Addition with Regrouping

Use a tens and ones chart to add. Shade the ones column yellow.
Shade the tens column orange.

tens ones

| 7 | 5 | | 3 | 2 | | 5 | 5 | | 6 | 1 | | 2 | 2 |
| + | 9 | | + 3 | 8 | | + 1 | 7 | | + 2 | 9 | | + | 8 |

| 4 | 8 | | 3 | 8 | | 2 | 9 | | 2 | 9 | | 4 | 6 |
| + 3 | 8 | | + 4 | 5 | | + 6 | 9 | | + 5 | 4 | | + 4 | 6 |

| 1 | 7 | | 1 | 3 | | 3 | 7 | | 5 | 8 | | 4 | 5 |
| + 5 | 7 | | + 7 | 9 | | + 3 | 6 | | + 2 | 9 | | + 1 | 7 |

| 2 | 6 | | 5 | 5 | | 3 | 5 | | 2 | 7 | | 7 | 6 |
| + 2 | 8 | | + 3 | 9 | | + 3 | 5 | | + 6 | 7 | | + | 5 |

| 3 | 7 | | 1 | 9 | | 5 | 4 | | 3 | 8 | | 2 | 4 |
| + 4 | 3 | | + 2 | 3 | | + 3 | 8 | | + 1 | 9 | | + 2 | 7 |

Why did the farmer name his pig Ink?

___ ___ ___   ___ ___ ___ ___ | ___ ___
91 62 41   40 47 46 62 | 52 62

___ ___ ___ ___ | ___ ___ ___ ___ ___ ___ ___ |
71 62 43 70 | 61 47 94 94 66 94 63

___ ___ ___ | ___ ___ | ___ ___ ___ | ___ ___ ___ !
93 47 70 | 93 65 | 52 66 46 | 43 62 94

A	B	C	D	E	F
17 + 23	36 + 55	22 + 19	37 + 36	29 + 33	26 + 39

G	H	I	J	K	L
44 + 19	29 + 23	38 + 28	29 + 49	59 + 12	29 + 28

N	O	P	R	S	T
67 + 27	48 + 45	29 + 14	26 + 35	27 + 19	35 + 35

U	V
18 + 29	57 + 27

Watch out! Some letters are not used in the riddle.

Math Riddle: Two-Digit Addition with Regrouping

Why was the broom late?

__ __ | __ __ __ __ __ __ __ __ __ !
81 51 | 73 70 36 80 55 92 36 84 51

Watch out! Some letters are not used in the riddle.

A 14 + 28	B 13 + 49	C 39 + 11	D 38 + 8	E 19 + 17	G 28 + 32
H 66 + 9	I 63 + 18	J 54 + 7	K 36 + 58	L 48 + 9	M 59 + 19
N 57 + 6	O 24 + 49	P 57 + 27	R 34 + 46	S 28 + 27	T 16 + 35
U 49 + 42	V 35 + 35	W 66 + 26	X 19 + 76	Y 77 + 13	Z 24 + 47

Math Riddle: Two-Digit Addition with Regrouping

Why don't traffic lights go swimming?

___ ___ ___ ___ ___ ___ ___ | ___ ___ ___ ___ | ___ ___ ___ ___ | ___ ___ ___ |
92 70 38 20 73 55 70 | 61 71 70 84 | 61 20 60 70 | 61 42 42 |

___ ___ ___ ___ | ___ ___ | ___ ___ ___ ___ ___ ___ !
52 42 41 83 | 61 42 | 38 71 20 41 83 70

Watch out! Some letters are not used in the riddle.

A	B	C	D	E	F
19 + 1	63 + 29	29 + 9	74 + 19	45 + 25	69 + 18
G 58 + 25	**H** 57 + 14	**I** 45 + 36	**J** 78 + 8	**K** 34 + 26	**L** 26 + 26
M 43 + 7	**N** 28 + 13	**O** 35 + 7	**P** 47 + 47	**Q** 86 + 9	**R** 35 + 39
S 39 + 16	**T** 52 + 9	**U** 66 + 7	**V** 17 + 18	**W** 58 + 32	**Y** 67 + 17

Three-Digit Addition Without Regrouping

Line up the ones, tens, and hundreds.

Add the ones.

hundreds	tens	ones
2	2	3
+ 3	4	5
		8

Next add the tens.

hundreds	tens	ones
2	2	3
+ 3	4	5
	6	8

Then add the hundreds.

hundreds	tens	ones
2	2	3
+ 3	4	5
5	6	8

Use a hundreds, tens, and ones chart to add. Shade the ones column yellow. Shade the tens column orange. Shade the hundreds column green.

4	5	4
+ 2	3	1

1	2	2
+ 5	1	5

3	7	1
+ 3	2	7

1	3	5
+ 7	6	2

4	1	2
+ 5	5	0

7	2	3
+ 2	2	5

4	6	2
+ 2	2	3

2	8	4
+ 3	1	1

1	5	4
+ 8	3	3

2	3	1
+ 4	2	6

5	5	3
+ 3	1	1

7	6	2
+ 1	3	7

Three-Digit Addition Without Regrouping

Use a hundreds, tens, and ones chart to add. Shade the ones column yellow. Shade the tens column orange. Shade the hundreds column green.

	1	3	3
+		1	4

	6	5	5
+	1	3	0

	2	1	3
+	5	0	0

	1	5	5
+	3	2	3

	3	1	4
+		4	3

	7	2	3
+	2	0	5

	3	7	7
+	1	1	1

	4	3	2
+	4	2	2

	2	3	5
+	1	1	3

	4	7	2
+	1	2	6

	2	6	3
+	7	1	3

	2	5	4
+	3	1	2

	4	2	1
+	3	3	2

	1	1	6
+	2	6	0

	5	8	5
+	4	1	4

	5	4	3
+	4	3	6

Why did the reporter walk into the ice cream shop?

___ ___ ___ ___ ___ ___ ___ | ___ ___ | ___ ___ ___ ___ ___ ___ | ___ |
469 359 566 358 243 586 359 | 189 359 | 317 358 697 669 359 337 | 358 |

___ ___ ___ ___ ___ !
586 566 538 538 956

Watch out! Some letters are not used in the riddle.

A 121 + 237	B 123 + 346	C 134 + 432	D 212 + 125	E 246 + 113	F 255 + 524
H 152 + 37	I 313 + 154	J 266 + 112	K 155 + 341	L 171 + 528	M 284 + 215
N 516 + 181	O 321 + 217	P 524 + 432	Q 435 + 204	R 112 + 352	S 443 + 143
T 253 + 416	U 142 + 101	V 564 + 223	W 305 + 12	X 171 + 321	Y 416 + 120

Three-Digit Addition with Regrouping

Line up the ones, tens, and hundreds.
Add the ones.
Then add the tens.

If there are more than 9 tens,
trade 10 tens for 1 hundred.
Regroup in the hundreds column.
Write the tens.
Add the hundreds.

hundreds	tens	ones
^{1}3	3	6
+ 2	9	3
6	2	9

Trade 10 tens from 120 for 1 hundred.
Regroup by writing 1 in the hundreds column.

Use a hundreds, tens, and ones chart to add. Shade the ones column yellow. Shade the tens column orange. Shade the hundreds column green.

☐				☐				☐				☐		
5	6	4		2	2	2		1	7	5		4	3	9
+ 2	5	5		+ 4	9	1		+ 2	1	6		+ 2	9	0

☐				☐				☐				☐		
2	1	2		3	7	6		5	6	4		4	2	9
+ 1	9	5		+ 4	4	1		+ 2	7	1		+ 1	8	0

Three-Digit Addition with Regrouping

Use a hundreds, tens, and ones chart to add. Hint: If there are more than 9 ones, trade 10 ones for 1 ten. Regroup in the tens column.

2 3 9 + 4 1 2 **6 5 1**	3 7 8 + 3 1 9	4 6 4 + 2 1 6	6 5 7 + 1 5 4

2 3 6 + 3 9 8	8 2 4 + 8 6	5 8 3 + 2 8 9	7 7 7 + 1 6 4

Add. Regroup in the tens column and the hundreds column.

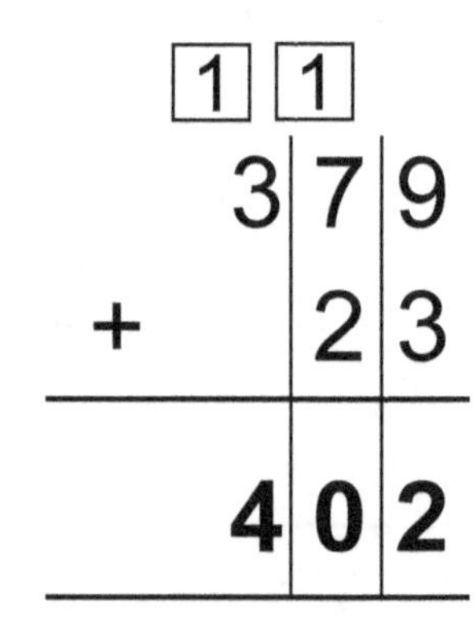

3 7 9 + 2 3 **4 0 2**	2 8 7 + 1 2 8	4 5 7 + 1 6 6	5 6 4 + 2 5 7

How do you catch a squirrel?

638 367 603 546 449 | 569 328 | 364 | 583 592 576 576 | 364 243 500 |

364 638 583 | 367 603 661 576 | 364 | 243 569 583 !

Watch out! Some letters are not used in the riddle.

A 119 + 245	**B** 180 + 269	**C** 258 + 380	**D** 173 + 327	**E** 458 + 118	**F** 397 + 352
G 249 + 314	**H** 296 + 292	**I** 382 + 221	**J** 402 + 168	**K** 415 + 246	**L** 138 + 229
M 385 + 161	**N** 138 + 105	**O** 284 + 275	**P** 192 + 136	**Q** 463 + 244	**R** 337 + 255
S 208 + 342	**T** 144 + 439	**U** 272 + 297	**V** 339 + 333	**W** 216 + 347	**Y** 115 + 316

Why did the student eat his homework?

Watch out! Some letters are not used in the riddle.

___ ___ ___ | ___ ___ ___ ___ ___ ___ ___ | ___ ___ ___ ___ | ___ ___
728 518 856 | 728 856 415 824 518 856 318 | 957 415 693 928 | 693 728

___ ___ ___ | ___ | ___ ___ ___ ___ ___ | ___ ___ | ___ ___ ___ ___ !
837 415 957 | 415 | 519 693 856 824 856 | 791 658 | 824 415 645 856

A	B	C	D	E	F
193 + 222	184 + 130	451 + 373	664 + 264	272 + 584	465 + 193

G	H	I	J	K	L
386 + 305	223 + 295	507 + 186	184 + 271	328 + 317	535 + 182

M	N	O	P	R	S
676 + 118	289 + 208	367 + 424	250 + 269	148 + 170	629 + 328

T	U	V	W	Y	Z
561 + 167	770 + 177	182 + 409	441 + 396	333 + 281	412 + 295

Addition Test 1—Sums to 10

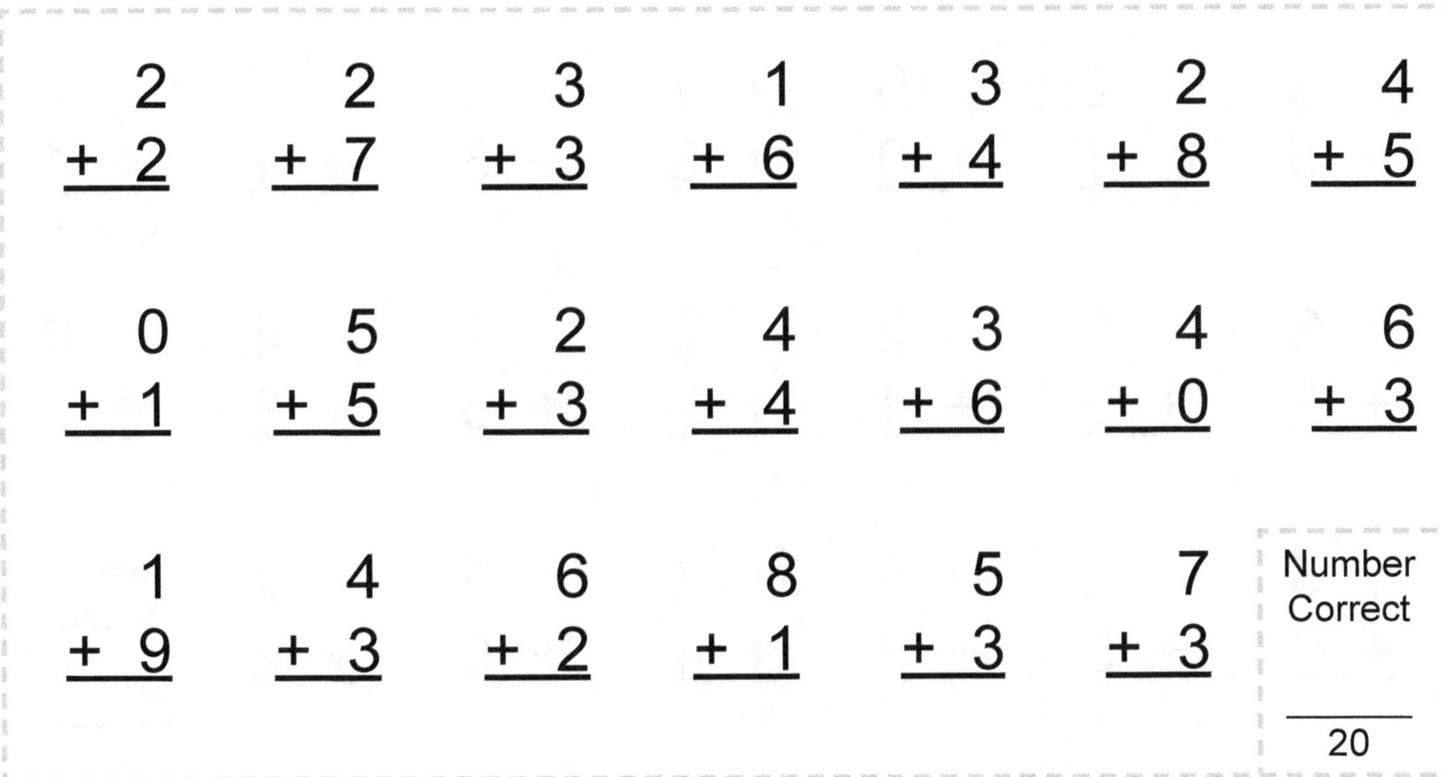

$$\begin{array}{cccccc}
6 & 8 & 2 & 3 & 4 & 5 & 1 \\
+\ 3 & +\ 2 & +\ 4 & +\ 6 & +\ 3 & +\ 1 & +\ 2 \\
\end{array}$$

$$\begin{array}{cccccc}
1 & 10 & 4 & 2 & 5 & 4 & 2 \\
+\ 1 & +\ 0 & +\ 1 & +\ 7 & +\ 2 & +\ 5 & +\ 6 \\
\end{array}$$

$$\begin{array}{cccccc}
3 & 1 & 0 & 4 & 5 & 4 \\
+\ 3 & +\ 9 & +\ 4 & +\ 6 & +\ 4 & +\ 4 \\
\end{array}$$

Number Correct

___
20

Addition Test 2—Sums to 10

$$\begin{array}{ccccccc}
2 & 2 & 3 & 1 & 3 & 2 & 4 \\
+\ 2 & +\ 7 & +\ 3 & +\ 6 & +\ 4 & +\ 8 & +\ 5 \\
\end{array}$$

$$\begin{array}{ccccccc}
0 & 5 & 2 & 4 & 3 & 4 & 6 \\
+\ 1 & +\ 5 & +\ 3 & +\ 4 & +\ 6 & +\ 0 & +\ 3 \\
\end{array}$$

$$\begin{array}{cccccc}
1 & 4 & 6 & 8 & 5 & 7 \\
+\ 9 & +\ 3 & +\ 2 & +\ 1 & +\ 3 & +\ 3 \\
\end{array}$$

Number Correct

___
20

Addition Test 3—Sums to 10

3	2	0	3	7	5	4
+ 3	+ 6	+ 9	+ 4	+ 3	+ 1	+ 6
5	1	2	5	6	0	7
+ 5	+ 9	+ 0	+ 3	+ 3	+ 5	+ 2
8	1	0	4	3	3	
+ 2	+ 7	+ 1	+ 3	+ 1	+ 7	

Number Correct

____
20

Addition Test 4—Sums to 10

3	2	10	1	4	7	4
+ 5	+ 1	+ 0	+ 8	+ 5	+ 1	+ 4
3	0	2	2	4	4	9
+ 2	+ 9	+ 4	+ 2	+ 6	+ 3	+ 1
3	2	6	1	5	7	
+ 7	+ 5	+ 3	+ 4	+ 5	+ 2	

Number Correct

____
20

Addition Test 5—Sums to 10

6 + 3	8 + 1	2 + 3	3 + 6	4 + 0	5 + 1	3 + 2
1 + 2	2 + 0	4 + 1	1 + 7	5 + 2	4 + 6	2 + 6
4 + 3	1 + 9	0 + 5	2 + 6	5 + 4	2 + 4	

Number Correct

———
20

Addition Test 6—Sums to 10

2 + 2	2 + 6	0 + 8	4 + 1	3 + 0	2 + 5	4 + 3
3 + 4	7 + 2	6 + 3	0 + 6	3 + 6	4 + 0	5 + 3
1 + 9	5 + 5	4 + 4	8 + 2	3 + 3	2 + 1	

Number Correct

———
20

Addition Test 7—Sums to 10

6 + 3	1 + 5	9 + 0	3 + 4	5 + 4	1 + 1	4 + 4
2 + 0	1 + 9	3 + 3	2 + 2	7 + 3	0 + 3	1 + 8
6 + 2	8 + 2	5 + 3	3 + 2	2 + 1	4 + 5	Number Correct 20

Addition Test 8—Sums to 10

3 + 5	4 + 6	5 + 5	2 + 6	1 + 4	2 + 1	4 + 4
9 + 1	0 + 8	6 + 3	3 + 3	2 + 2	8 + 2	3 + 2
3 + 7	5 + 2	4 + 5	1 + 2	5 + 4	7 + 2	Number Correct 20

Addition Test 9—Sums to 10

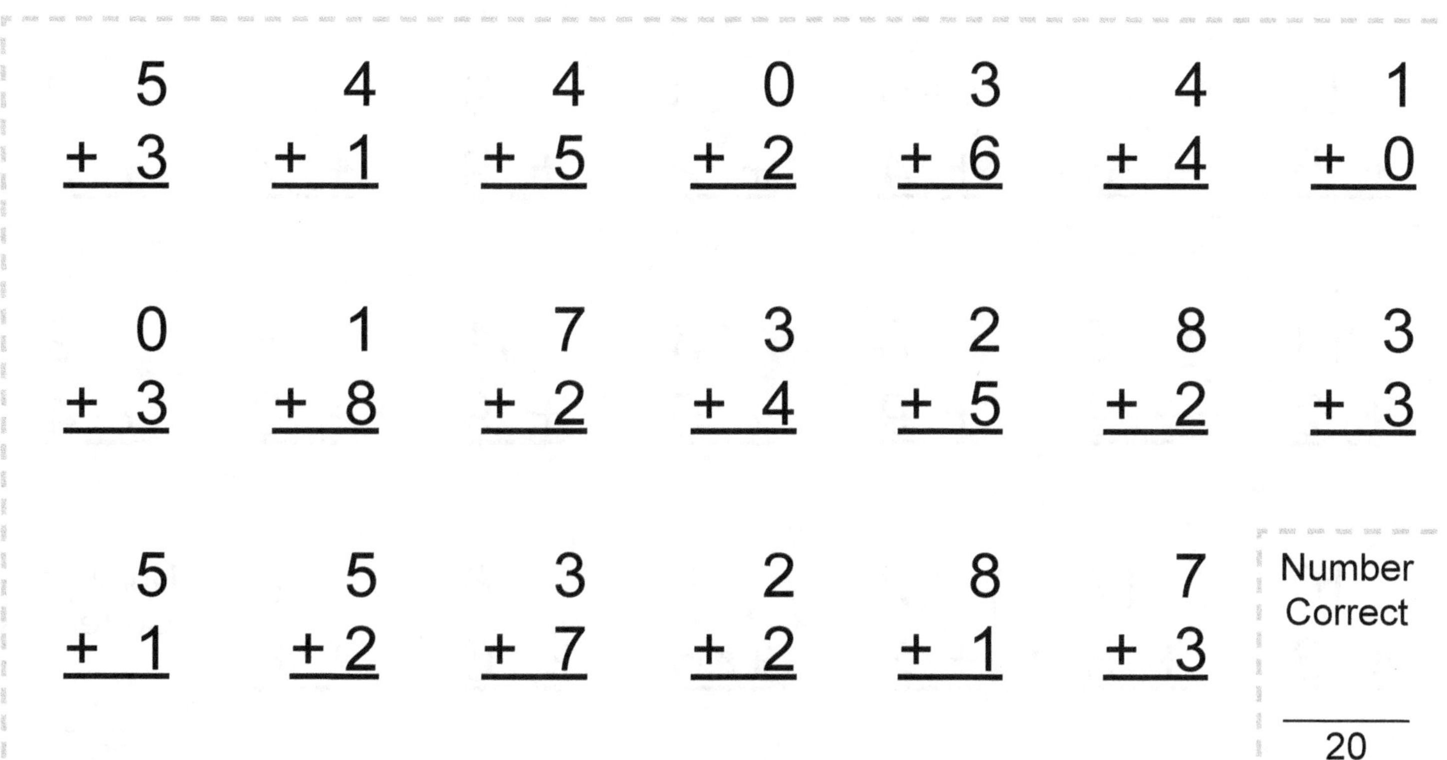

2	2	1	3	4	5	3
+ 7	+ 5	+ 2	+ 4	+ 2	+ 5	+ 3

2	4	6	7	6	1	8
+ 8	+ 4	+ 2	+ 3	+ 3	+ 1	+ 2

3	0	5	3	4	4
+ 2	+ 6	+ 4	+ 5	+ 0	+ 6

Number Correct ___ / 20

Addition Test 10—Sums to 10

5	4	4	0	3	4	1
+ 3	+ 1	+ 5	+ 2	+ 6	+ 4	+ 0

0	1	7	3	2	8	3
+ 3	+ 8	+ 2	+ 4	+ 5	+ 2	+ 3

5	5	3	2	8	7
+ 1	+ 2	+ 7	+ 2	+ 1	+ 3

Number Correct ___ / 20

Addition Test 1—Sums from 11 to 20

13 + 2	7 + 7	3 + 10	7 + 8	8 + 6	6 + 5	5 + 9
7 + 5	8 + 9	9 + 3	6 + 9	17 + 1	10 + 6	9 + 10
10 + 8	18 + 2	8 + 4	5 + 8	6 + 6	9 + 7	Number Correct ______ 20

Addition Test 2—Sums from 11 to 20

11 + 5	12 + 6	10 + 4	3 + 9	9 + 9	6 + 7	8 + 5
14 + 2	5 + 9	8 + 9	13 + 5	11 + 9	8 + 8	9 + 4
10 + 8	17 + 3	12 + 3	5 + 6	6 + 6	8 + 6	Number Correct ______ 20

Addition Test 3—Sums from 11 to 20

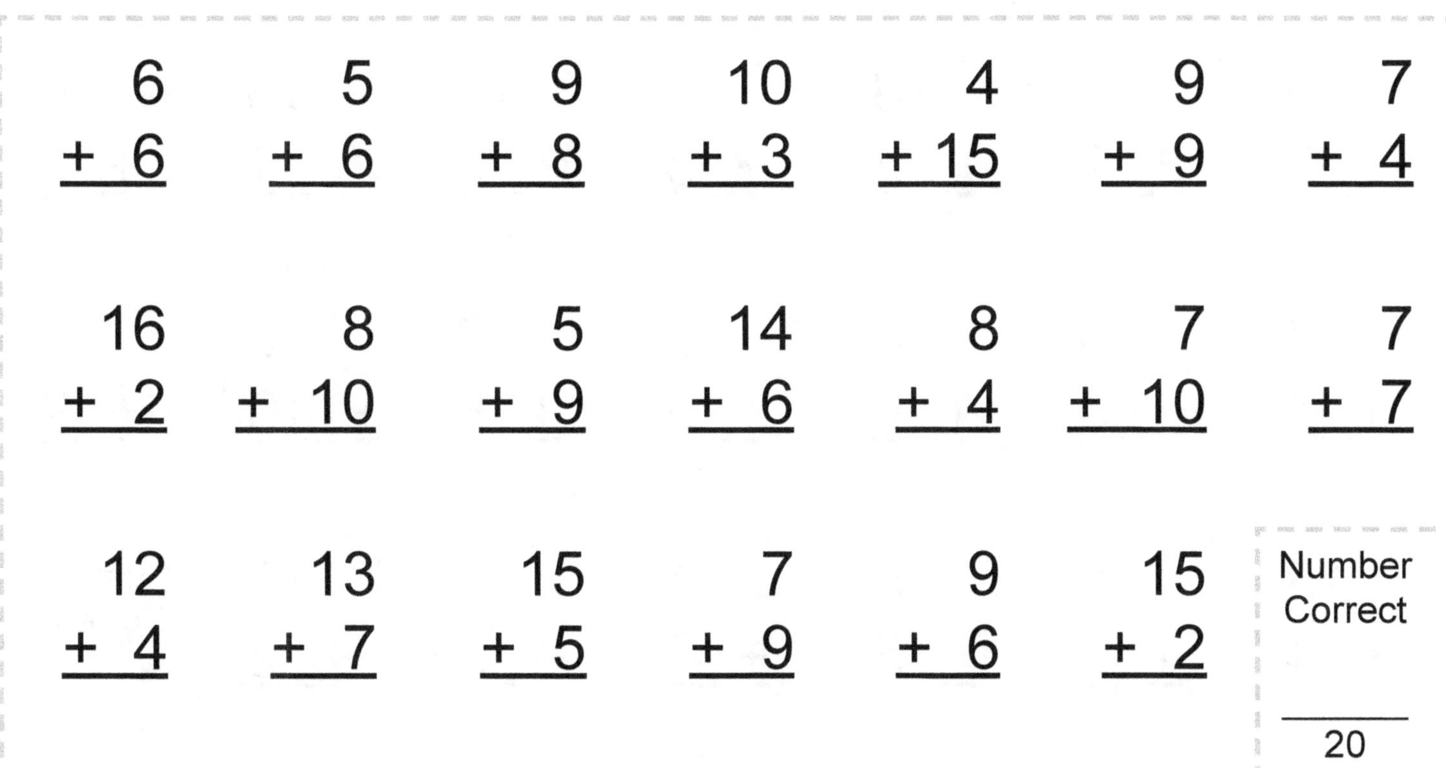

13	9	10	12	6	12	7
+ 6	+ 3	+ 4	+ 8	+ 6	+ 3	+ 6

15	11	16	9	9	10	17
+ 5	+ 2	+ 1	+ 9	+ 5	+ 5	+ 2

8	9	6	9	14	8
+ 9	+ 7	+ 5	+ 6	+ 6	+ 8

Number Correct

______
20

Addition Test 4—Sums from 11 to 20

6	5	9	10	4	9	7
+ 6	+ 6	+ 8	+ 3	+ 15	+ 9	+ 4

16	8	5	14	8	7	7
+ 2	+ 10	+ 9	+ 6	+ 4	+ 10	+ 7

12	13	15	7	9	15
+ 4	+ 7	+ 5	+ 9	+ 6	+ 2

Number Correct

______
20

Addition Test 5—Sums from 11 to 20

11	8	4	10	9	6	8
+ 9	+ 7	+ 9	+ 8	+ 6	+ 5	+ 6

5	11	16	9	6	10	17
+ 15	+ 2	+ 4	+ 9	+ 7	+ 5	+ 2

18	5	10	7	13	7
+ 2	+ 7	+ 4	+ 8	+ 2	+ 7

Number Correct

_____

20

Addition Test 6—Sums from 11 to 20

6	13	16	10	14	19	9
+ 6	+ 7	+ 2	+ 3	+ 5	+ 1	+ 2

13	9	6	7	8	6	9
+ 2	+ 10	+ 9	+ 5	+ 8	+ 10	+ 9

16	11	8	7	10	10
+ 4	+ 3	+ 5	+ 4	+ 9	+ 2

Number Correct

_____

20

Addition Test 7—Sums from 11 to 20

2	8	17	10	9	6	15
+ 9	+ 7	+ 2	+ 8	+ 6	+ 5	+ 3

5	11	16	9	6	10	4
+ 8	+ 9	+ 1	+ 9	+ 7	+ 5	+ 8

8	5	10	7	13	7
+ 8	+ 7	+ 4	+ 8	+ 7	+ 7

Number Correct

____
20

Addition Test 8—Sums from 11 to 20

11	6	9	17	14	9	13
+ 5	+ 8	+ 2	+ 3	+ 5	+ 7	+ 6

10	6	8	4	4	7	4
+ 2	+ 6	+ 9	+ 10	+ 8	+ 10	+ 7

13	12	3	7	8	15
+ 4	+ 8	+ 9	+ 9	+ 3	+ 2

Number Correct

____
20

Addition Test 9—Sums from 11 to 20

2 + 10	8 + 8	19 + 1	10 + 5	4 + 8	6 + 5	5 + 7
5 + 15	11 + 2	16 + 1	9 + 2	4 + 7	9 + 5	17 + 2
3 + 9	9 + 6	10 + 8	16 + 4	13 + 2	8 + 5	Number Correct ――― 20

Addition Test 10—Sums from 11 to 20

7 + 6	15 + 5	12 + 8	20 + 0	4 + 7	8 + 6	14 + 2
13 + 5	6 + 10	9 + 9	12 + 4	8 + 3	7 + 7	11 + 7
14 + 4	10 + 1	8 + 5	9 + 7	6 + 6	15 + 4	Number Correct ――― 20

Addition Test 1—Two-Digit Addition Without Regrouping

61	72	40	63	84	55	30
+ 24	+ 15	+ 59	+ 24	+ 13	+ 21	+ 42

14	16	42	34	20	40	33
+ 61	+ 73	+ 44	+ 23	+ 60	+ 42	+ 56

75	16	55	11	80	27
+ 24	+ 82	+ 32	+ 66	+ 19	+ 60

Number Correct

______
20

Addition Test 2—Two-Digit Addition Without Regrouping

55	72	30	23	54	46	26
+ 34	+ 13	+ 42	+ 55	+ 34	+ 31	+ 12

41	32	20	35	16	21	35
+ 48	+ 57	+ 37	+ 44	+ 22	+ 78	+ 63

26	72	17	21	60	14
+ 23	+ 24	+ 72	+ 17	+ 39	+ 64

Number Correct

______
20

Addition Test 3—Two-Digit Addition Without Regrouping

10	82	20	13	24	45	16
+ 64	+ 17	+ 69	+ 74	+ 33	+ 54	+ 43

30	10	16	13	40	10	11
+ 59	+ 10	+ 82	+ 25	+ 49	+ 39	+ 58

47	13	24	15	52	38
+ 31	+ 13	+ 40	+ 73	+ 26	+ 61

Number Correct

_____
20

Addition Test 4—Two-Digit Addition Without Regrouping

38	82	37	23	34	49	13
+ 20	+ 17	+ 61	+ 74	+ 34	+ 50	+ 73

55	16	30	26	10	40	14
+ 44	+ 23	+ 55	+ 23	+ 16	+ 49	+ 52

83	60	31	12	35	16
+ 11	+ 28	+ 37	+ 86	+ 44	+ 62

Number Correct

_____
20

Addition Test 5—Two-Digit Addition Without Regrouping

80 + 14	42 + 42	60 +31	53 + 44	24 + 63	35 + 44	76 + 12
30 + 59	10 + 26	16 + 82	13 + 24	40 + 49	10 + 43	11 + 57
55 + 31	45 + 13	22 + 40	16 + 63	42 + 20	18 + 11	Number Correct ___ 20

Addition Test 6—Two-Digit Addition Without Regrouping

68 + 20	18 + 21	40 + 51	23 + 64	34 + 34	49 + 30	13 + 43
85 + 14	66 + 33	40 + 45	26 + 13	10 + 56	32 + 62	54 + 12
73 + 12	50 + 48	41 + 27	32 + 26	25 + 34	27 + 42	Number Correct ___ 20

Addition Test 7—Two-Digit Addition Without Regrouping

14 + 61	81 + 16	25 + 12	14 + 83	23 + 30	22 + 74	31 + 62
39 + 50	13 + 26	12 + 86	13 + 51	46 + 40	15 + 40	14 + 50
46 + 33	16 + 11	23 + 45	14 + 74	56 + 22	31 + 48	

Number Correct

———
20

Addition Test 8—Two-Digit Addition Without Regrouping

33 + 42	24 + 71	45 +53	11 + 84	27 + 11	53 + 40	13 + 61
55 + 30	29 + 20	30 + 45	26 + 62	10 + 36	20 + 72	44 + 44
13 + 54	60 + 27	31 + 35	12 + 75	35 + 22	16 + 80	

Number Correct

———
20

Addition Test 9—Two-Digit Addition Without Regrouping

61	72	20	63	84	56	30
+ 24	+ 15	+ 69	+ 24	+ 13	+ 21	+ 42

14	16	42	34	20	47	33
+ 61	+ 73	+ 44	+ 23	+ 60	+ 42	+ 56

75	16	55	11	80	27	Number Correct
+ 24	+ 82	+ 32	+ 66	+ 19	+ 60	

Number Correct ___ / 20

Addition Test 10—Two-Digit Addition Without Regrouping

22	63	47	89	16	34	55
+ 74	+ 23	+ 12	+ 10	+ 82	+ 61	+ 14

80	71	62	53	24	25	16
+ 14	+ 26	+ 35	+ 44	+ 23	+ 72	+ 60

32	43	10	29	73	85	Number Correct
+ 23	+ 24	+ 79	+ 20	+ 15	+ 4	

Number Correct ___ / 20

Addition Test 1—Two-Digit Addition with Regrouping

48	77	26	16	48	49	17
+ 36	+ 18	+16	+ 75	+ 49	+ 44	+ 47

22	47	17	33	17	31	16
+ 28	+ 34	+ 27	+ 39	+ 44	+ 59	+ 27

46	14	16	15	43	18
+ 27	+ 19	+ 54	+ 67	+ 28	+ 66

Number Correct

____
20

Addition Test 2—Two-Digit Addition with Regrouping

35	68	44	19	35	66	46
+ 47	+ 5	+ 29	+ 38	+ 57	+ 17	+ 29

38	63	35	49	74	69	14
+ 8	+ 19	+ 55	+ 26	+ 17	+ 19	+ 57

26	17	11	18	54	25
+ 66	+ 56	+ 39	+ 67	+ 27	+ 68

Number Correct

____
20

Addition Test 3—Two-Digit Addition with Regrouping

37	66	29	47	24	45	6
+ 54	+ 17	+ 59	+ 44	+ 29	+ 39	+ 78

36	18	16	13	45	17	11
+ 59	+ 25	+ 67	+ 9	+ 47	+ 48	+ 59

47	18	29	17	55	38	Number Correct
+ 36	+ 18	+ 41	+ 73	+ 36	+ 42	

____

20

Addition Test 4—Two-Digit Addition with Regrouping

38	73	65	44	37	49	13
+ 26	+ 17	+ 29	+ 46	+ 34	+ 22	+ 78

35	19	33	24	15	46	17
+ 45	+ 24	+ 58	+ 57	+ 16	+ 49	+ 56

79	67	39	18	35	18	Number Correct
+ 11	+ 28	+ 39	+ 47	+ 46	+ 62	

____

20

Addition Test 5—Two-Digit Addition with Regrouping

55	87	54	7	64	45	48
+ 37	+ 7	+ 18	+ 67	+ 19	+ 25	+ 23

56	27	76	24	49	15	19
+ 39	+ 49	+ 18	+ 36	+ 43	+ 55	+ 51

47	48	29	18	37	29
+ 36	+ 44	+ 51	+ 63	+ 53	+ 42

Number Correct

______
20

Addition Test 6—Two-Digit Addition with Regrouping

58	77	49	26	37	28	13
+ 26	+ 13	+ 24	+ 45	+ 36	+ 58	+ 79

56	29	55	36	17	18	59
+ 26	+ 23	+ 39	+ 34	+ 27	+ 44	+ 26

85	63	17	38	65	18
+ 9	+ 28	+ 36	+ 47	+ 6	+ 62

Number Correct

______
20

Addition Test 7—Two-Digit Addition with Regrouping

45	38	2	67	89	46	72
+ 36	+ 57	+ 59	+ 24	+ 6	+ 49	+ 18

24	37	14	43	15	49	68
+ 59	+ 29	+ 78	+ 47	+ 49	+ 19	+ 13

47	18	29	17	55	38
+ 36	+ 18	+ 41	+ 73	+ 36	+ 42

Number Correct

______
20

Addition Test 8—Two-Digit Addition with Regrouping

38	73	65	44	34	49	17
+ 26	+ 17	+ 29	+ 46	+ 38	+ 23	+ 75

46	22	38	57	68	74	19
+ 45	+ 29	+ 58	+ 29	+ 16	+ 9	+ 55

77	88	9	17	36	19
+ 18	+ 8	+ 49	+ 28	+ 36	+ 42

Number Correct

______
20

Addition Test 9—Two-Digit Addition with Regrouping

32	66	29	47	24	45	16
+ 18	+ 17	+ 59	+ 44	+ 67	+ 39	+ 78

36	17	16	13	45	17	13
+ 55	+ 29	+ 56	+ 79	+ 47	+ 46	+ 57

47	18	29	17	56	38
+ 36	+ 18	+ 41	+ 73	+ 36	+ 42

Number Correct

_____
20

Addition Test 10—Two-Digit Addition with Regrouping

44	77	31	84	76	9	26
+ 26	+ 17	+ 49	+ 7	+ 16	+ 65	+ 39

35	19	33	24	15	49	17
+ 45	+ 29	+ 58	+ 29	+ 16	+ 46	+ 56

49	67	39	18	35	18
+ 11	+ 28	+ 39	+ 67	+ 46	+ 63

Number Correct

_____
20

Addition Test 1—Three-Digit Addition Without Regrouping

301	372	410	163	180	205	131
+ 304	+ 115	+ 569	+ 524	+ 115	+ 211	+ 741

814	216	742	234	820	340	333
+ 161	+ 673	+ 144	+ 723	+ 160	+ 342	+ 156

275	113	555	211	180	222	Number Correct
+ 204	+ 180	+ 432	+ 160	+ 319	+ 613	

20

Addition Test 2—Three-Digit Addition Without Regrouping

505	272	120	235	851	246	211
+ 240	+ 713	+ 422	+ 151	+ 135	+ 431	+ 120

411	300	200	365	316	201	305
+ 438	+ 532	+ 317	+ 404	+ 322	+ 718	+ 603

422	732	125	131	610	140	Number Correct
+ 240	+ 244	+ 271	+ 107	+ 349	+ 654	

20

Addition Test 3—Three-Digit Addition Without Regrouping

110	820	320	313	254	425	186
+ 604	+ 127	+ 615	+ 114	+ 313	+ 554	+ 403

130	790	116	123	400	120	117
+ 549	+ 100	+ 182	+ 250	+ 469	+ 361	+ 860

147	103	124	715	652	130
+ 341	+ 133	+ 740	+ 273	+126	+ 160

Number Correct ______ 20

Addition Test 4—Three-Digit Addition Without Regrouping

380	420	307	203	835	349	615
+ 200	+ 117	+ 651	+ 794	+ 130	+ 250	+ 371

500	112	730	211	180	494	314
+ 470	+ 230	+ 255	+ 280	+ 106	+ 400	+ 532

283	160	314	112	301	160
+ 110	+ 128	+ 130	+ 826	+ 412	+ 632

Number Correct ______ 20

Addition Test 5—Three-Digit Addition Without Regrouping

150 + 100	192 + 402	210 + 731	253 + 244	124 + 663	305 + 434	700 + 112
333 + 530	160 + 126	611 + 280	213 + 724	140 + 435	210 + 432	131 + 527
505 + 391	454 + 140	122 + 401	316 + 163	142 + 250	118 + 111	Number Correct ______ 20

Addition Test 6—Three-Digit Addition Without Regrouping

618 + 120	217 + 220	340 + 531	231 + 604	131 + 340	249 + 300	713 + 243
850 + 149	653 + 330	430 + 245	126 + 813	101 + 567	320 + 622	542 + 100
703 + 122	500 + 441	141 + 211	342 + 246	206 + 310	201 + 142	Number Correct ______ 20

Addition Test 7—Three-Digit Addition Without Regrouping

114	821	253	144	523	227	310
+ 601	+ 126	+ 132	+ 423	+ 350	+ 742	+ 602

339	132	210	113	546	105	114
+ 350	+ 260	+ 681	+251	+ 440	+ 400	+ 150

476	618	222	314	356	331
+ 313	+ 160	+ 452	+ 374	+ 232	+ 103

Number Correct

______

20

Addition Test 8—Three-Digit Addition Without Regrouping

313	233	452	111	427	453	510
+ 402	+ 711	+523	+ 243	+ 141	+ 410	+ 361

305	296	360	261	101	220	468
+ 350	+ 600	+ 125	+ 621	+ 236	+ 742	+ 410

100	680	231	512	235	160
+ 154	+ 217	+ 235	+ 375	+ 242	+ 330

Number Correct

______

20

Addition Test 9—Three-Digit Addition Without Regrouping

761	692	220	262	834	540	230
+ 124	+ 105	+ 629	+ 210	+ 133	+ 251	+ 542

214	116	412	314	120	247	323
+ 331	+ 523	+ 474	+ 213	+ 860	+ 642	+ 500

105	215	651	619	800	207	Number Correct
+ 234	+ 110	+ 330	+ 260	+ 109	+ 620	

———
20

Addition Test 10—Three-Digit Addition Without Regrouping

212	603	447	189	605	134	755
+ 774	+ 243	+ 142	+ 210	+ 223	+ 761	+ 114

860	761	162	203	424	205	112
+ 104	+ 210	+ 835	+ 184	+ 423	+ 792	+ 860

320	243	110	322	673	130	Number Correct
+ 233	+ 124	+ 179	+ 120	+ 215	+ 221	

———
20

Addition Test 1—Three-Digit Addition with Regrouping

197	276	396	436	588	679	787
+ 276	+ 238	+ 266	+ 289	+ 249	+ 246	+ 147

682	597	496	383	277	152	599
+ 128	+ 132	+ 127	+ 431	+ 354	+ 259	+ 199

591	494	376	285	343	168
+ 221	+ 419	+ 354	+ 268	+ 378	+ 166

Number Correct

_____
20

Addition Test 2—Three-Digit Addition with Regrouping

185	267	349	483	594	665	777
+ 257	+ 279	+ 189	+ 438	+ 357	+ 176	+ 129

736	669	535	449	374	269	184
+ 191	+ 183	+ 271	+ 226	+ 434	+ 549	+ 651

366	467	391	588	154	222
+ 166	+ 256	+ 339	+ 267	+ 657	+ 189

Number Correct

_____
20

Addition Test 3—Three-Digit Addition with Regrouping

331	466	569	148	594	145	776
+ 188	+ 197	+ 59	+ 404	+ 227	+ 689	+ 178

131	708	216	183	445	286	571
+ 399	+ 129	+ 188	+ 327	+ 489	+ 349	+ 159

447	398	299	377	252	138	Number Correct
+ 236	+ 218	+ 501	+ 473	+ 676	+ 172	

___
20

Addition Test 4—Three-Digit Addition with Regrouping

244	377	191	284	171	199	126
+ 191	+ 117	+ 409	+ 517	+ 119	+ 615	+ 499

155	119	673	174	115	486	267
+ 185	+ 129	+ 58	+ 199	+ 396	+ 489	+ 686

289	367	439	218	435	518	Number Correct
+ 211	+ 328	+ 439	+ 187	+ 346	+ 163	

___
20

Addition Test 5—Three-Digit Addition with Regrouping

688	767	398	87	853	162	537
+ 40	+ 107	+ 315	+ 594	+ 98	+ 777	+ 168

119	229	648	208	154	91	571
+ 199	+ 189	+ 188	+ 344	+ 489	+ 791	+ 290

539	661	341	189	224	67	
+ 235	+ 299	+ 388	+ 142	+ 176	+ 744	Number Correct

20

Addition Test 6—Three-Digit Addition with Regrouping

425	340	290	228	533	203	61
+ 191	+ 273	+ 453	+ 417	+ 288	+ 559	+ 459

106	477	583	663	475	234	899
+ 685	+ 329	+ 58	+ 199	+ 397	+ 199	+ 77

393	479	690	328	544	185	
+ 55	+ 489	+ 287	+ 484	+ 346	+ 167	Number Correct

20

Addition Test 7—Three-Digit Addition with Regrouping

582	463	299	386	53	668	439
+ 48	+ 108	+ 375	+ 494	+ 398	+ 77	+ 108

518	279	248	408	254	82	575
+ 194	+ 188	+ 197	+ 344	+ 489	+ 631	+ 308

136	377	127	184	253	67	Number Correct
+ 236	+ 253	+ 399	+ 147	+ 198	+ 685	

20

Addition Test 8—Three-Digit Addition with Regrouping

465	380	230	217	596	205	99
+ 261	+ 383	+ 583	+ 697	+ 308	+ 659	+ 889

106	27	533	643	455	264	748
+ 685	+ 799	+ 188	+ 299	+ 377	+ 168	+ 77

693	379	590	328	865	289	Number Correct
+ 44	+ 591	+ 372	+ 209	+ 46	+ 267	

20

Addition Test 9—Three-Digit Addition with Regrouping

779	263	288	345	79	125	869
+ 58	+ 109	+ 545	+ 294	+ 438	+ 89	+ 108

686	215	224	408	232	41	555
+ 194	+ 188	+ 197	+ 343	+ 489	+ 691	+ 307

176	379	167	148	254	38	Number Correct
+ 232	+ 259	+ 369	+ 184	+ 117	+ 785	

———
20

Addition Test 10—Three-Digit Addition with Regrouping

485	360	230	217	596	105	99
+ 381	+ 463	+ 583	+ 607	+ 378	+ 789	+ 881

626	27	193	153	445	264	778
+ 185	+ 799	+ 588	+ 299	+ 377	+ 168	+ 82

663	399	580	318	825	239	Number Correct
+ 53	+ 298	+ 377	+ 206	+ 45	+ 264	

———
20

How Am I Doing?

Sums to 10 (pages 61–65)

Number Correct	Test 1	Test 2	Test 3	Test 4	Test 5	Test 6	Test 7	Test 8	Test 9	Test 10
20										
19										
18										
17										
16										
15										
14										
13										
12										
11										
10										
9										
8										
7										
6										
5										
4										
3										
2										
1										

Sums from 11 to 20 (pages 66–70)

Number Correct	Test 1	Test 2	Test 3	Test 4	Test 5	Test 6	Test 7	Test 8	Test 9	Test 10
20										
19										
18										
17										
16										
15										
14										
13										
12										
11										
10										
9										
8										
7										
6										
5										
4										
3										
2										
1										

Two-Digit Addition Without Regrouping (pages 71–75)

Number Correct	Test 1	Test 2	Test 3	Test 4	Test 5	Test 6	Test 7	Test 8	Test 9	Test 10
20										
19										
18										
17										
16										
15										
14										
13										
12										
11										
10										
9										
8										
7										
6										
5										
4										
3										
2										
1										

Two-Digit Addition with Regrouping (pages 76–80)

Number Correct	Test 1	Test 2	Test 3	Test 4	Test 5	Test 6	Test 7	Test 8	Test 9	Test 10
20										
19										
18										
17										
16										
15										
14										
13										
12										
11										
10										
9										
8										
7										
6										
5										
4										
3										
2										
1										

How Am I Doing?

Three-Digit Addition Without Regrouping (pages 81–85)

Number Correct	Test 1	Test 2	Test 3	Test 4	Test 5	Test 6	Test 7	Test 8	Test 9	Test 10
20										
19										
18										
17										
16										
15										
14										
13										
12										
11										
10										
9										
8										
7										
6										
5										
4										
3										
2										
1										

Three-Digit Addition with Regrouping (pages 86–90)

Number Correct	Test 1	Test 2	Test 3	Test 4	Test 5	Test 6	Test 7	Test 8	Test 9	Test 10
20										
19										
18										
17										
16										
15										
14										
13										
12										
11										
10										
9										
8										
7										
6										
5										
4										
3										
2										
1										

FANTASTIC WORK!

Name

Answers

Sums to 5 (page 2)

Use the blocks to add.

4 + 1 = **5**   2 + 3 = **5**

1 + 1 = **2**   2 + 2 = **4**

1 + 4 = **5**   3 + 2 = **5**

3 + 1 = **4**   1 + 2 = **3**

1 + 3 = **4**   2 + 1 = **3**

Sums to 5 (page 3)

Draw ● s to help you add.

1 + 2 = **3**   2 + 3 = **5**

3 + 1 = **4**   1 + 4 = **5**

1 + 3 = **4**   2 + 1 = **3**

2 + 2 = **4**   1 + 1 = **2**

3 + 2 = **5**   4 + 1 = **5**

Sums to 5 (page 4)

Use the key to color the picture.

Color Key
1 – yellow
2 – orange
3 – green
4 – blue
5 – red

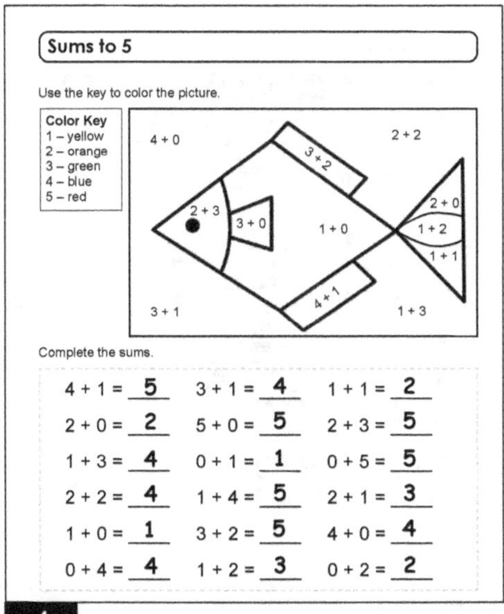

Complete the sums.

4 + 1 = **5**   3 + 1 = **4**   1 + 1 = **2**
2 + 0 = **2**   5 + 0 = **5**   2 + 3 = **5**
1 + 3 = **4**   0 + 1 = **1**   0 + 5 = **5**
2 + 2 = **4**   1 + 4 = **5**   2 + 1 = **3**
1 + 0 = **1**   3 + 2 = **5**   4 + 0 = **4**
0 + 4 = **4**   1 + 2 = **3**   0 + 2 = **2**

Addition Facts for 2, 3, 4, and 5 (page 5)

Use the key to color the picture.

Color Key
2 – red
3 – blue
4 – green
5 – yellow

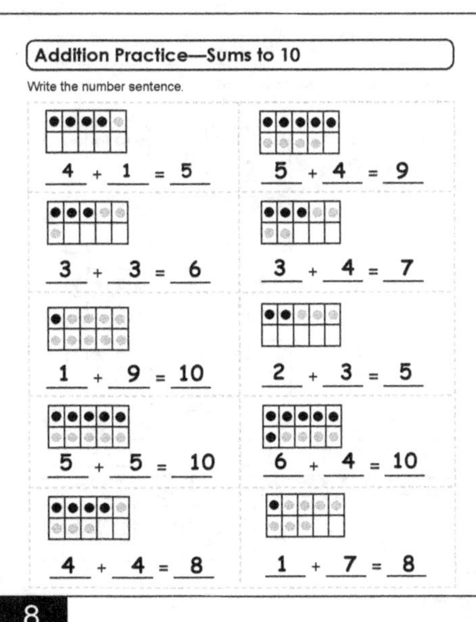

Complete the facts.

0 + 5 = **5**   1 + 1 = **2**   4 + 0 = **4**
1 + 2 = **3**   4 + 1 = **5**   2 + 0 = **2**
1 + 4 = **5**   0 + 4 = **4**   2 + 3 = **5**
0 + 3 = **3**   2 + 2 = **4**   0 + 2 = **2**
3 + 2 = **5**   3 + 1 = **4**   5 + 0 = **5**
2 + 1 = **3**   1 + 3 = **4**   3 + 0 = **3**

Addition Facts for 6, 7, 8, and 9 (page 6)

Use the key to color the picture.

Color Key
6 – red
7 – blue
8 – green
9 – yellow

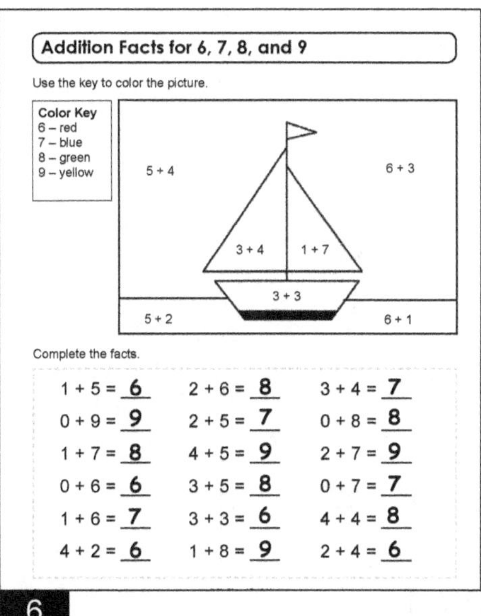

Complete the facts.

1 + 5 = **6**   2 + 6 = **8**   3 + 4 = **7**
0 + 9 = **9**   2 + 5 = **7**   0 + 8 = **8**
1 + 7 = **8**   4 + 5 = **9**   2 + 7 = **9**
0 + 6 = **6**   3 + 5 = **8**   0 + 7 = **7**
1 + 6 = **7**   3 + 3 = **6**   4 + 4 = **8**
4 + 2 = **6**   1 + 8 = **9**   2 + 4 = **6**

How Many Ways Can You Make 10? (page 7)

Use the ten frames to make 10. Use two different colors. Then, write the answers.

4 + **6** = **10**

Answers might vary. Sample answers:

5 + **5** = **10**

7 + **3** = **10**

8 + **2** = **10**

9 + **1** = **10**

10 + **0** = **10**

Addition Practice—Sums to 10 (page 8)

Write the number sentence.

4 + 1 = 5   5 + 4 = 9

3 + 3 = 6   3 + 4 = 7

1 + 9 = 10   2 + 3 = 5

5 + 5 = 10   6 + 4 = 10

4 + 4 = 8   1 + 7 = 8

Addition Practice—Sums to 10 (page 9)

Write the number sentence.

3 + 6 = 9   1 + 1 = 2

8 + 1 = 9   1 + 3 = 4

2 + 2 = 4   2 + 1 = 3

7 + 3 = 10   3 + 1 = 4

9 + 1 = 10   2 + 7 = 9

Panel 10 — Add 1 or 2 by Counting On

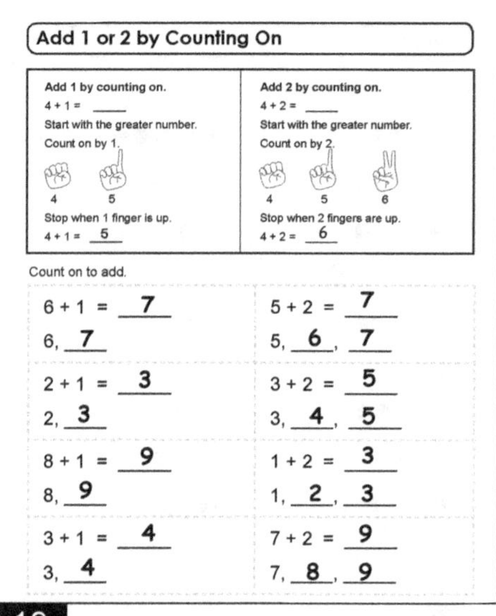

Add 1 by counting on.
4 + 1 = ____
Start with the greater number.
Count on by 1.
4   5
Stop when 1 finger is up.
4 + 1 = 5

Add 2 by counting on.
4 + 2 = ____
Start with the greater number.
Count on by 2.
4   5   6
Stop when 2 fingers are up.
4 + 2 = 6

Count on to add.

6 + 1 = 7
6, 7

5 + 2 = 7
5, 6, 7

2 + 1 = 3
2, 3

3 + 2 = 5
3, 4, 5

8 + 1 = 9
8, 9

1 + 2 = 3
1, 2, 3

3 + 1 = 4
3, 4

7 + 2 = 9
7, 8, 9

Panel 11 — Add 1 or 2 by Counting On

Count on to add.

4 + 1 = 5
4, 5

2 + 2 = 4
2, 3, 4

9 + 1 = 10
9, 10

4 + 2 = 6
4, 5, 6

7 + 1 = 8
7, 8

8 + 2 = 10
8, 9, 10

1 + 1 = 2
1, 2

6 + 2 = 8
6, 7, 8

5 + 1 = 6
5, 6

0 + 2 = 2
0, 1, 2

0 + 1 = 1
0, 1

9 + 2 = 11
9, 10, 11

Panel 12 — Use a Number Line to Add

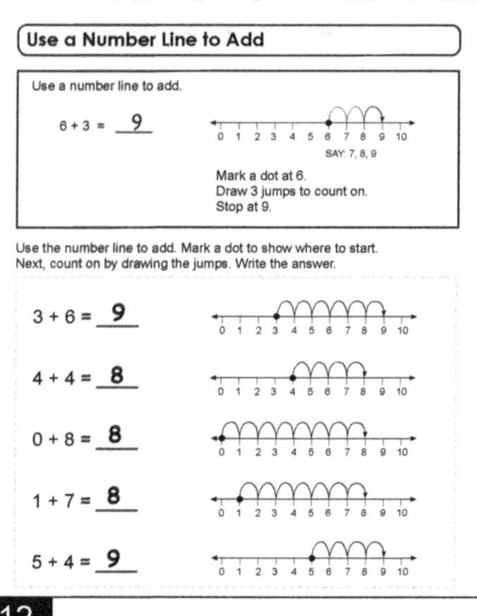

Use a number line to add.

6 + 3 = 9
0 1 2 3 4 5 6 7 8 9 10
SAY: 7, 8, 9

Mark a dot at 6.
Draw 3 jumps to count on.
Stop at 9.

Use the number line to add. Mark a dot to show where to start.
Next, count on by drawing the jumps. Write the answer.

3 + 6 = 9
4 + 4 = 8
0 + 8 = 8
1 + 7 = 8
5 + 4 = 9

Panel 13 — Use a Number Line to Add

Use the number line to add by counting on. Mark a dot to show
where to start. Next, draw the jumps. Write the answer.

0 + 7 = 7
8 + 2 = 10
9 + 1 = 10
2 + 6 = 8
4 + 3 = 7
1 + 8 = 9
3 + 3 = 6
2 + 4 = 6

Panel 14 — Make Addition Sentences

Show three ways

Answers might vary. Sample answers:

4 + 5 = 9
7 + 2 = 9
6 + 3 = 9

1 + 2 = 3
2 + 1 = 3
0 + 3 = 3

4 + 3 = 7
2 + 5 = 7
1 + 6 = 7

2 + 3 = 5
1 + 4 = 5
3 + 2 = 5

Panel 15 — Make Addition Sentences

Show three ways

Answers might vary. Sample answers:

2 + 8 = 10
7 + 3 = 10
5 + 5 = 10

2 + 6 = 8
7 + 1 = 8
5 + 3 = 8

2 + 4 = 6
3 + 3 = 6
1 + 5 = 6

2 + 2 = 4
1 + 3 = 4
3 + 1 = 4

Panel 16 — Numbers Can Be Added in Any Order

5 + 2 = 7
2 + 5 = 7

Use the ten frames to show adding numbers in two ways.
Use two different colors. Then, write the answers.

6 + 2 = 8
2 + 6 = 8

3 + 4 = 7
4 + 3 = 7

1 + 8 = 9
8 + 1 = 9

4 + 5 = 9
5 + 4 = 9

7 + 2 = 9
2 + 7 = 9

Panel 17 — Numbers Can Be Added in Any Order

Use the ten frames to show adding numbers in two ways.
Use two different colors. Then, write the answers.

6 + 4 = 10
4 + 6 = 10

2 + 3 = 5
3 + 2 = 5

1 + 7 = 8
7 + 1 = 8

5 + 3 = 8
3 + 5 = 8

1 + 3 = 4
3 + 1 = 4

Answers might vary. Sample answers: than 10.

8 + 2 = 2 + 8

Panel 18 — Addition Practice—Sums to 10

Use the key to color the picture.

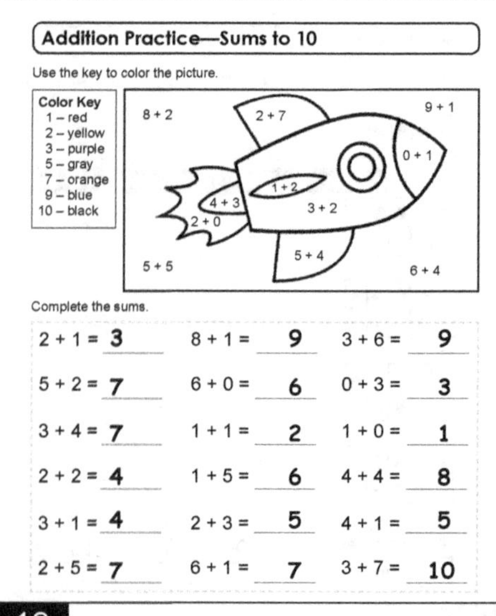

Complete the sums.

2 + 1 = 3
8 + 1 = 9
3 + 6 = 9

5 + 2 = 7
6 + 0 = 6
0 + 3 = 3

3 + 4 = 7
1 + 1 = 2
1 + 0 = 1

2 + 2 = 4
1 + 5 = 6
4 + 4 = 8

3 + 1 = 4
2 + 3 = 5
4 + 1 = 5

2 + 5 = 7
6 + 1 = 7
3 + 7 = 10

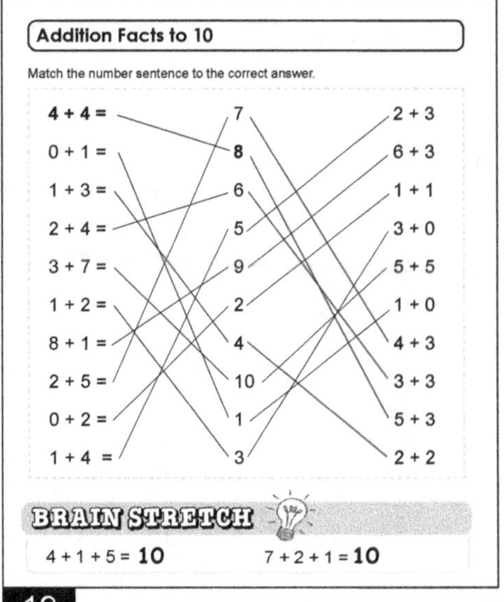

Addition Facts to 10

Match the number sentence to the correct answer.

4 + 4 =	7	2 + 3
0 + 1 =	8	6 + 3
1 + 3 =	6	1 + 1
2 + 4 =	5	3 + 0
3 + 7 =	9	5 + 5
1 + 2 =	2	1 + 0
8 + 1 =	4	4 + 3
2 + 5 =	10	3 + 3
0 + 2 =	1	5 + 3
1 + 4 =	3	2 + 2

BRAIN STRETCH

4 + 1 + 5 = **10**   7 + 2 + 1 = **10**

19

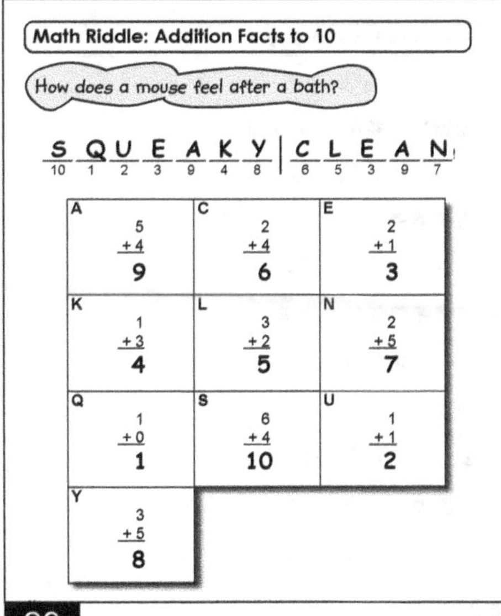

Math Riddle: Addition Facts to 10

How does a mouse feel after a bath?

$$\underset{10}{S}\ \underset{1}{Q}\ \underset{2}{U}\ \underset{3}{E}\ \underset{9}{A}\ \underset{4}{K}\ \underset{8}{Y}\ \Big|\ \underset{6}{C}\ \underset{5}{L}\ \underset{3}{E}\ \underset{9}{A}\ \underset{7}{N}$$

A	C	E
5 +4 **9**	2 +4 **6**	2 +1 **3**
K	**L**	**N**
1 +3 **4**	3 +2 **5**	2 +5 **7**
Q	**S**	**U**
1 +0 **1**	6 +4 **10**	1 +1 **2**
Y		
3 +5 **8**		

20

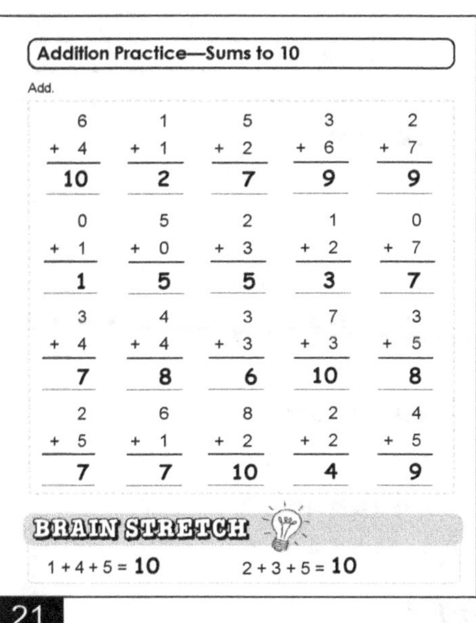

Addition Practice—Sums to 10

Add.

6 + 4 **10**	1 + 1 **2**	5 + 2 **7**	3 + 6 **9**	2 + 7 **9**
0 + 1 **1**	5 + 0 **5**	2 + 3 **5**	1 + 2 **3**	0 + 7 **7**
3 + 4 **7**	4 + 4 **8**	3 + 3 **6**	7 + 3 **10**	3 + 5 **8**
2 + 5 **7**	6 + 1 **7**	8 + 2 **10**	2 + 2 **4**	4 + 5 **9**

BRAIN STRETCH

1 + 4 + 5 = **10**   2 + 3 + 5 = **10**

21

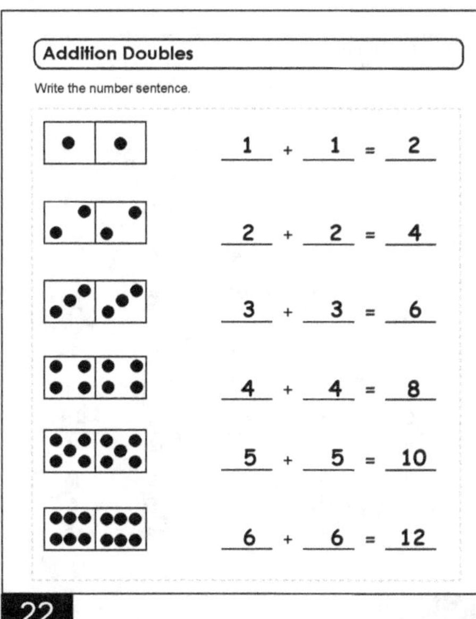

Addition Doubles

Write the number sentence.

_1_ + _1_ = _2_

_2_ + _2_ = _4_

_3_ + _3_ = _6_

_4_ + _4_ = _8_

_5_ + _5_ = _10_

_6_ + _6_ = _12_

22

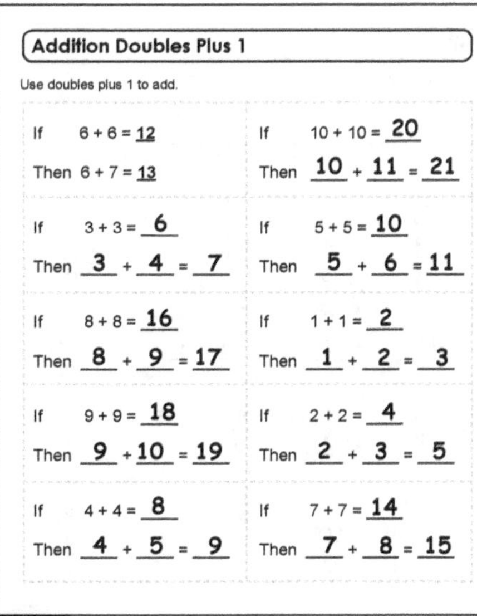

Addition Doubles Plus 1

Use doubles plus 1 to add.

If 6 + 6 = **12**   If 10 + 10 = **20**
Then 6 + 7 = **13**   Then **10** + **11** = **21**

If 3 + 3 = **6**   If 5 + 5 = **10**
Then **3** + **4** = **7**   Then **5** + **6** = **11**

If 8 + 8 = **16**   If 1 + 1 = **2**
Then **8** + **9** = **17**   Then **1** + **2** = **3**

If 9 + 9 = **18**   If 2 + 2 = **4**
Then **9** + **10** = **19** Then **2** + **3** = **5**

If 4 + 4 = **8**   If 7 + 7 = **14**
Then **4** + **5** = **9**   Then **7** + **8** = **15**

23

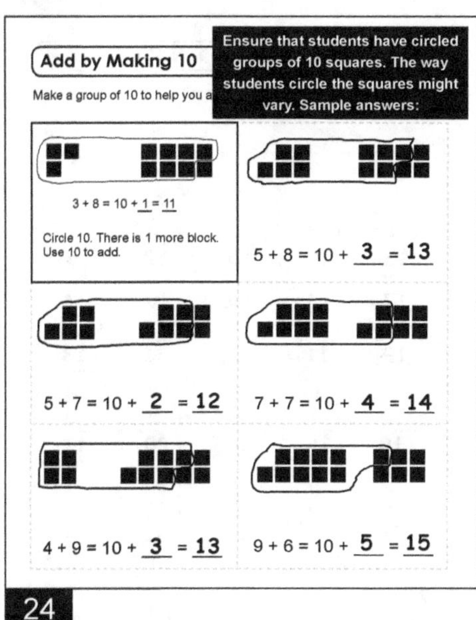

Add by Making 10

Ensure that students have circled groups of 10 squares. The way students circle the squares might vary. Sample answers:

Make a group of 10 to help you a...

3 + 8 = 10 + _1_ = _11_
Circle 10. There is 1 more block.
Use 10 to add.

5 + 8 = 10 + _3_ = **13**

5 + 7 = 10 + _2_ = **12**   7 + 7 = 10 + _4_ = **14**

4 + 9 = 10 + _3_ = **13**   9 + 6 = 10 + _5_ = **15**

24

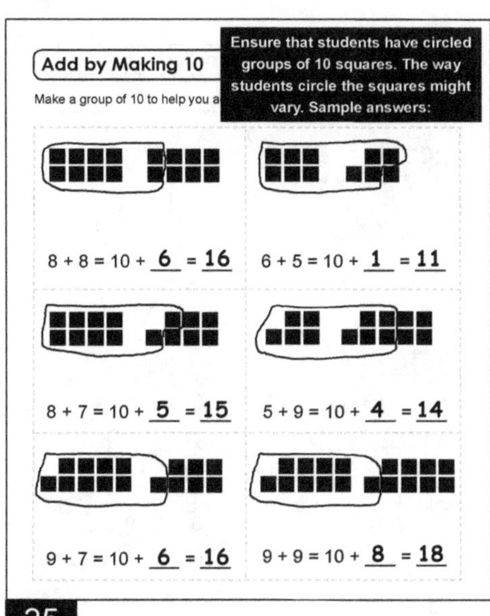

Add by Making 10

Ensure that students have circled groups of 10 squares. The way students circle the squares might vary. Sample answers:

Make a group of 10 to help you a...

8 + 8 = 10 + _6_ = **16**   6 + 5 = 10 + _1_ = **11**

8 + 7 = 10 + _5_ = **15**   5 + 9 = 10 + _4_ = **14**

9 + 7 = 10 + _6_ = **16**   9 + 9 = 10 + _8_ = **18**

25

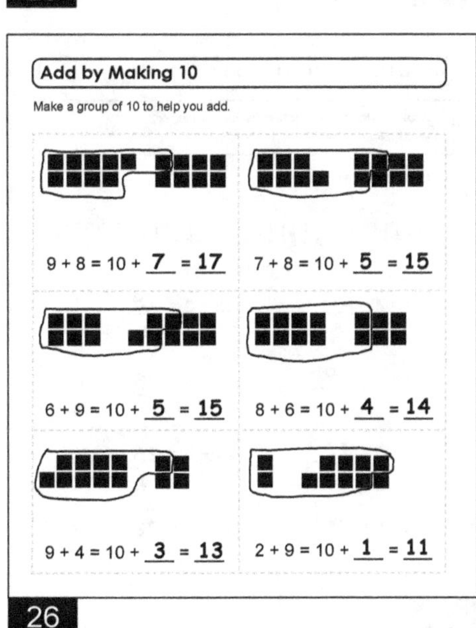

Add by Making 10

Make a group of 10 to help you add.

9 + 8 = 10 + _7_ = **17**   7 + 8 = 10 + _5_ = **15**

6 + 9 = 10 + _5_ = **15**   8 + 6 = 10 + _4_ = **14**

9 + 4 = 10 + _3_ = **13**   2 + 9 = 10 + _1_ = **11**

26

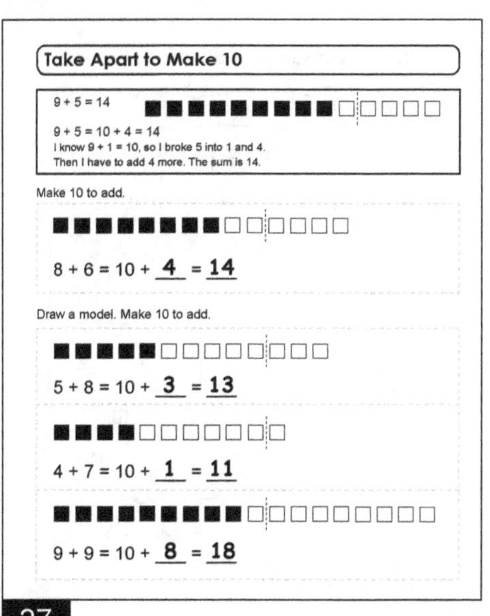

Take Apart to Make 10

9 + 5 = 14
9 + 5 = 10 + 4 = 14
I know 9 + 1 = 10, so I broke 5 into 1 and 4.
Then I have to add 4 more. The sum is 14.

Make 10 to add.

8 + 6 = 10 + _4_ = **14**

Draw a model. Make 10 to add.

5 + 8 = 10 + _3_ = **13**

4 + 7 = 10 + _1_ = **11**

9 + 9 = 10 + _8_ = **18**

27

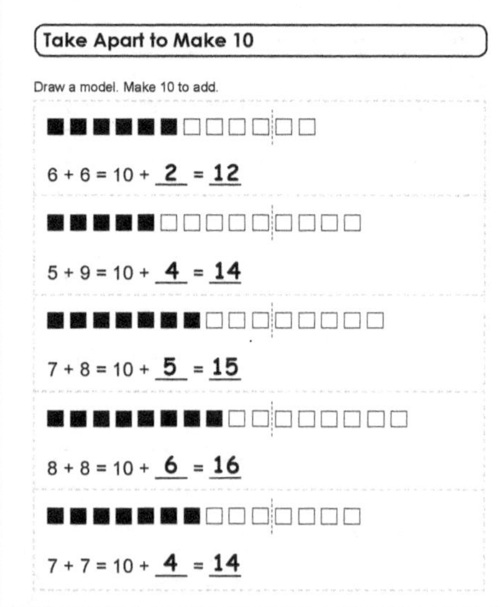
Take Apart to Make 10

Draw a model. Make 10 to add.

6 + 6 = 10 + 2 = 12
5 + 9 = 10 + 4 = 14
7 + 8 = 10 + 5 = 15
8 + 8 = 10 + 6 = 16
7 + 7 = 10 + 4 = 14

28

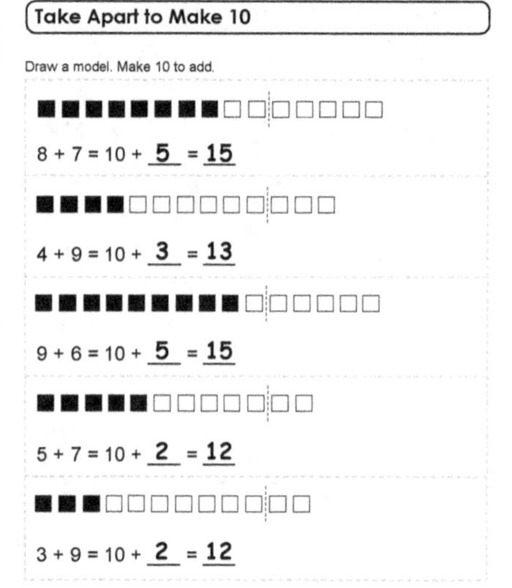
Take Apart to Make 10

Draw a model. Make 10 to add.

8 + 7 = 10 + 5 = 15
4 + 9 = 10 + 3 = 13
9 + 6 = 10 + 5 = 15
5 + 7 = 10 + 2 = 12
3 + 9 = 10 + 2 = 12

29

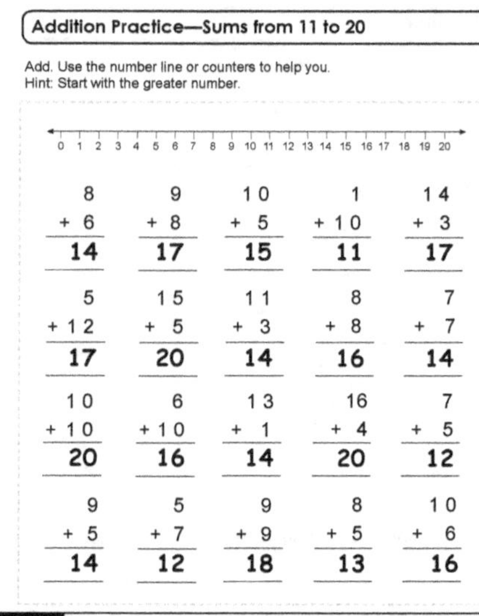
Addition Practice—Sums from 11 to 20

Add. Use the number line or counters to help you.
Hint: Start with the greater number.

0 1 2 3 4 5 6 7 8 9 10 11 12 13 14 15 16 17 18 19 20

8   9   10   1   14
+ 6   + 8   + 5   + 10   + 3
14   17   15   11   17

5   15   11   8   7
+ 12   + 5   + 3   + 8   + 7
17   20   14   16   14

10   6   13   16   7
+ 10   + 10   + 1   + 4   + 5
20   16   14   20   12

9   5   9   8   10
+ 5   + 7   + 9   + 5   + 6
14   12   18   13   16

30

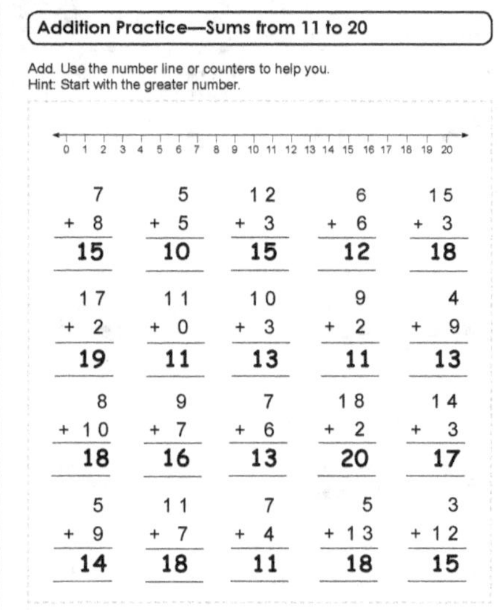
Addition Practice—Sums from 11 to 20

Add. Use the number line or counters to help you.
Hint: Start with the greater number.

0 1 2 3 4 5 6 7 8 9 10 11 12 13 14 15 16 17 18 19 20

7   5   12   6   15
+ 8   + 5   + 3   + 6   + 3
15   10   15   12   18

17   11   10   9   4
+ 2   + 0   + 3   + 2   + 9
19   11   13   11   13

8   9   7   18   14
+ 10   + 7   + 6   + 2   + 3
18   16   13   20   17

5   11   7   5   3
+ 9   + 7   + 4   + 13   + 12
14   18   11   18   15

31

Missing Numbers

Fill in the missing number. Use the number line to help you.

0 1 2 3 4 5 6 7 8 9 10 11 12 13 14 15 16 17 18 19 20

3   9   3   8   4
+ 3   + 9   + 9   + 6   + 11
6   18   12   14   15

9   9   7   6   10
+ 8   + 2   + 5   + 7   + 9
17   11   12   13   19

3   7   8   5   1
+ 2   + 0   + 10   + 9   + 10
5   7   18   14   11

8   10   6   2   10
+ 8   + 10   + 4   + 4   + 5
16   20   10   6   15

32

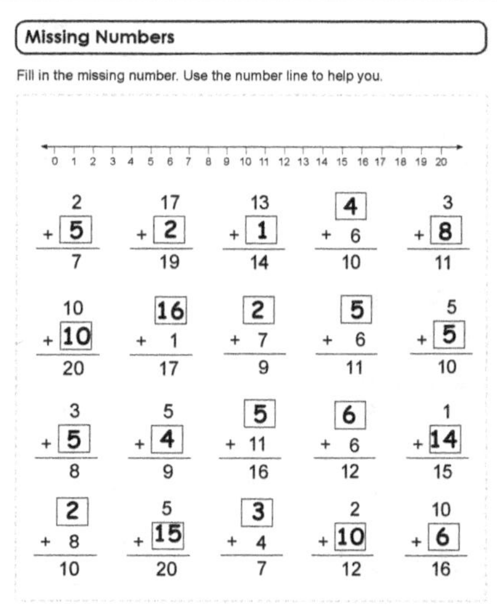
Missing Numbers

Fill in the missing number. Use the number line to help you.

0 1 2 3 4 5 6 7 8 9 10 11 12 13 14 15 16 17 18 19 20

2   17   13   4   3
+ 5   + 2   + 1   + 6   + 8
7   19   14   10   11

10   16   2   5   5
+ 10   + 1   + 7   + 6   + 5
20   17   9   11   10

3   5   5   6   1
+ 5   + 4   + 11   + 6   + 14
8   9   16   12   15

2   5   3   2   10
+ 8   + 15   + 4   + 10   + 6
10   20   7   12   16

33

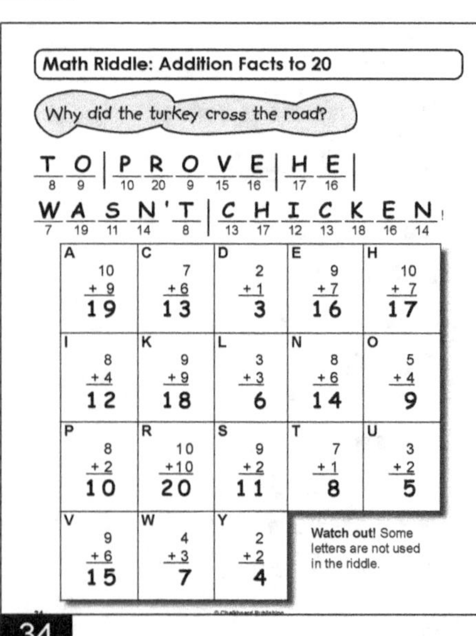
Math Riddle: Addition Facts to 20

Why did the turkey cross the road?

T O   P R O V E   H E
8 9   10 20 9 15 16 17 16

W A S N' T C H I C K E N
7 19 11 14 8 13 17 12 13 18 16 14

A   C   D   E   H
  10   7   2   9   10
  + 9   + 6   + 1   + 7   + 7
  19   13   3   16   17

I   K   L   N   O
  8   9   3   8   5
  + 4   + 9   + 3   + 6   + 4
  12   18   6   14   9

P   R   S   T   U
  8   10   9   7   3
  + 2   + 10   + 2   + 1   + 2
  10   20   11   8   5

V   W   Y
  9   4   2
  + 6   + 3   + 2
  15   7   4

Watch out! Some
letters are not used
in the riddle.

34

Use a Number Line to Add

You can find the sum of two numbers by counting on.
14 + 5 = 19   Count: 14, 15, 16, 17, 18, 19

Use the number line to find the sum.

0 1 2 3 4 5 6 7 8 9 10 11 12 13 14 15 16 17 18 19 20 21 22 23 24 25 26 27 28 29 30

24 + 4 = 28   15 + 3 = 18

24 + 5 = 29   16 + 9 = 25

5 + 12 = 17   21 + 5 = 26

18 + 5 = 23   15 + 7 = 22

35

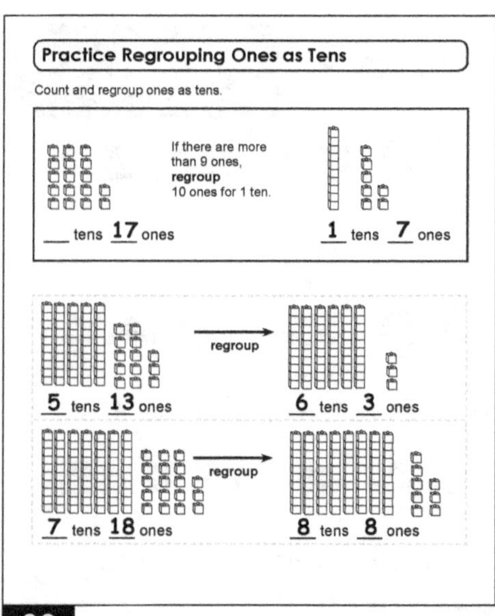
Practice Regrouping Ones as Tens

Count and regroup ones as tens.

If there are more
than 9 ones,
regroup
10 ones for 1 ten.

___ tens 17 ones   1 tens 7 ones

regroup
5 tens 13 ones   6 tens 3 ones

regroup
7 tens 18 ones   8 tens 8 ones

36

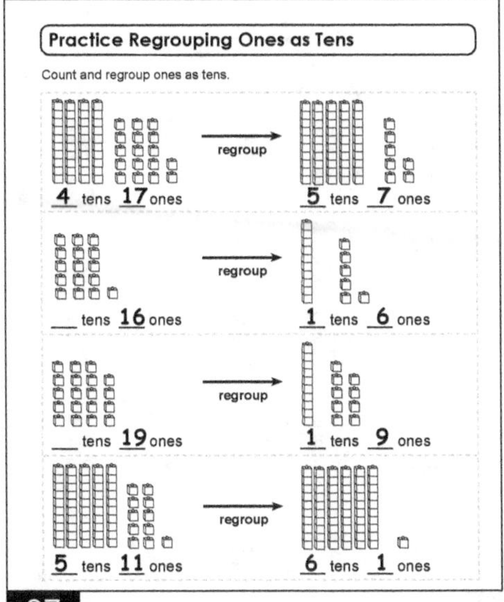

Practice Regrouping Ones as Tens

Count and regroup ones as tens.

4 tens **17** ones → regroup → **5** tens **7** ones

_____ tens **16** ones → regroup → **1** tens **6** ones

_____ tens **19** ones → regroup → **1** tens **9** ones

5 tens **11** ones → regroup → **6** tens **1** ones

37

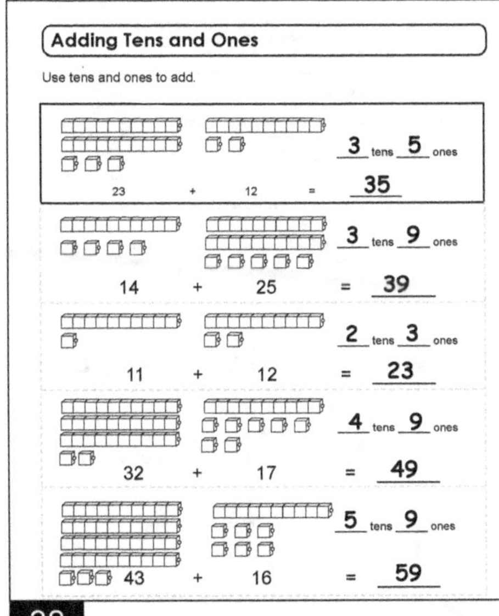

Adding Tens and Ones

Use tens and ones to add.

3 tens **5** ones
23 + 12 = **35**

3 tens **9** ones
14 + 25 = **39**

2 tens **3** ones
11 + 12 = **23**

4 tens **9** ones
32 + 17 = **49**

5 tens **9** ones
43 + 16 = **59**

38

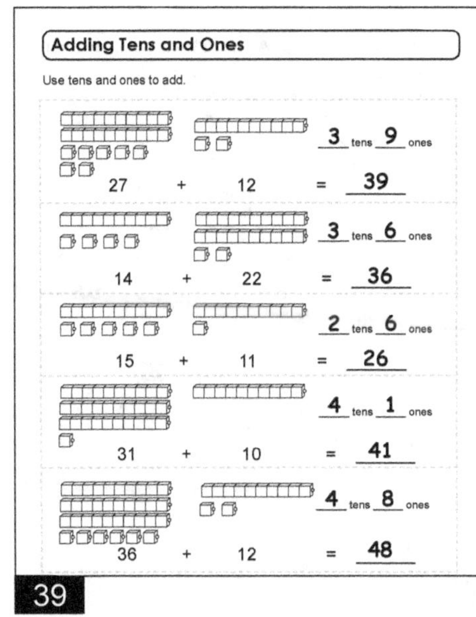

Adding Tens and Ones

Use tens and ones to add.

3 tens **9** ones
27 + 12 = **39**

3 tens **6** ones
14 + 22 = **36**

2 tens **6** ones
15 + 11 = **26**

4 tens **1** ones
31 + 10 = **41**

4 tens **8** ones
36 + 12 = **48**

39

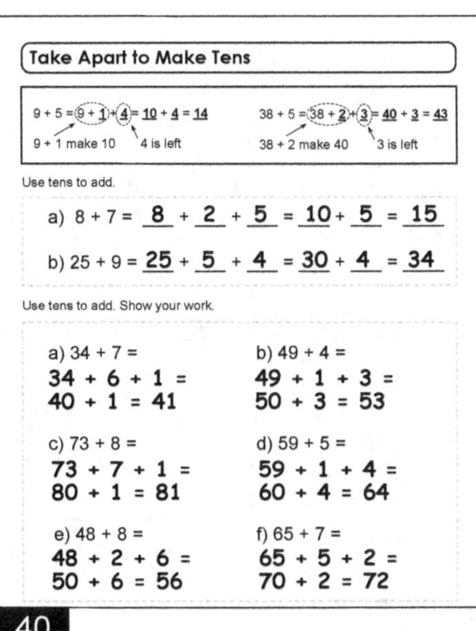

Take Apart to Make Tens

9 + 5 = (9 + 1) + 4 = 10 + 4 = 14   38 + 5 = (38 + 2) + 3 = 40 + 3 = 43
9 + 1 make 10   4 is left   38 + 2 make 40   3 is left

Use tens to add.

a) 8 + 7 = **8** + **2** + **5** = 10 + **5** = **15**

b) 25 + 9 = **25** + **5** + **4** = **30** + **4** = **34**

Use tens to add. Show your work.

a) 34 + 7 =
34 + 6 + 1 =
40 + 1 = 41

b) 49 + 4 =
49 + 1 + 3 =
50 + 3 = 53

c) 73 + 8 =
73 + 7 + 1 =
80 + 1 = 81

d) 59 + 5 =
59 + 1 + 4 =
60 + 4 = 64

e) 48 + 8 =
48 + 2 + 6 =
50 + 6 = 56

f) 65 + 7 =
65 + 5 + 2 =
70 + 2 = 72

40

Take Apart to Make Tens

Use tens to add. Show your work.

a) 16 + 8 =
16 + 4 + 4 =
20 + 4 = 24

b) 37 + 9 =
37 + 3 + 6 =
40 + 6 = 46

c) 63 + 9 =
63 + 7 + 2 =
70 + 2 = 72

d) 37 + 8 =
37 + 3 + 5 =
40 + 5 = 45

e) 44 + 7 =
44 + 6 + 1 =
50 + 1 = 51

f) 55 + 7 =
55 + 5 + 2 =
60 + 2 = 62

g) 62 + 9 =
62 + 8 + 1 =
70 + 1 = 71

h) 77 + 7 =
77 + 3 + 4 =
80 + 4 = 84

i) 17 + 6 =
17 + 3 + 3 =
20 + 3 = 23

j) 53 + 9 =
53 + 7 + 2 =
60 + 2 = 62

41

41

Two-Digit Addition Without Regrouping

Line up the ones and tens.

First add the ones.

tens	ones
2	3
+ 4	5
	8

Then add the tens.

tens	ones
2	3
+ 4	5
6	8

Use a tens and ones chart to add. Shade the ones column yellow. Shade the tens column orange.

tens	ones				
5	4	22	71	35	44
+ 3	1	+ 15	+ 27	+ 62	+ 30
8	5	37	98	97	74

1	2	76	62	84	33
+ 5	0	+ 12	+ 23	+ 11	+ 13
6	2	88	85	95	46

5	4	31	53	62	14
+ 3	3	+ 26	+ 11	+ 37	+ 30
8	7	57	64	99	44

8	2	12	34	20	52
+ 1	5	+ 40	+ 14	+ 13	+ 43
9	7	52	48	33	95

42

Two-Digit Addition Without Regrouping

Use a tens and ones chart to add. Shade the ones column yellow. Shade the tens column orange.

tens	ones				
8	3	13	36	21	53
+ 1	4	+ 43	+ 13	+ 32	+ 46
9	7	56	49	53	99

5	5	23	72	16	45
+ 3	0	+ 25	+ 26	+ 60	+ 32
8	5	48	98	76	77

1	3	77	63	85	34
+ 5	0	+ 11	+ 13	+ 14	+ 15
6	3	88	76	99	49

5	1	32	54	43	15
+ 2	1	+ 22	+ 12	+ 36	+ 33
7	2	54	66	79	48

7	2	24	46	11	82
+ 2	5	+ 32	+ 12	+ 55	+ 16
9	7	56	58	66	98

43

Two-Digit Addition Without Regrouping

Use a tens and ones chart to add. Shade the ones column yellow. Shade the tens column orange.

tens	ones				
2	5	44	72	16	47
+ 1	4	+ 41	+ 17	+ 30	+ 50
3	9	85	89	46	97

3	0	12	55	12	32
+ 3	1	+ 43	+ 32	+ 54	+ 46
6	1	55	87	66	78

6	3	24	45	71	12
+ 2	4	+ 34	+ 43	+ 22	+ 83
8	7	58	88	93	95

1	4	46	15	21	73
+ 7	4	+ 53	+ 42	+ 66	+ 12
8	8	99	57	87	85

8	3	13	35	21	53
+ 1	2	+ 45	+ 13	+ 38	+ 45
9	5	58	48	59	98

44

Two-Digit Addition Without Regrouping

Use a tens and ones chart to add. Shade the ones column yellow. Shade the tens column orange.

tens	ones				
9	5	32	55	61	22
+	3	+ 36	+ 14	+ 23	+ 4
9	8	68	69	84	26

4	8	33	21	22	42
+ 3	1	+ 45	+ 70	+ 54	+ 46
7	9	78	91	76	88

1	7	82	37	50	45
+ 5	2	+ 13	+ 30	+ 29	+ 13
6	9	95	67	79	58

7	6	55	33	21	70
+ 2	1	+ 23	+ 42	+ 67	+ 5
9	7	78	75	88	75

5	2	13	64	31	24
+ 4	7	+ 23	+ 34	+ 11	+ 25
9	9	36	98	42	49

45

46 — Math Riddle: Two-Digit Addition Without Regrouping

Why are snakes hard to fool?

T H E Y | H A V E | N O |
33 52 61 54 | 52 65 57 61 | 79 63

L E G S | T O | P U L L !
76 61 85 99 | 33 63 | 73 50 76 76

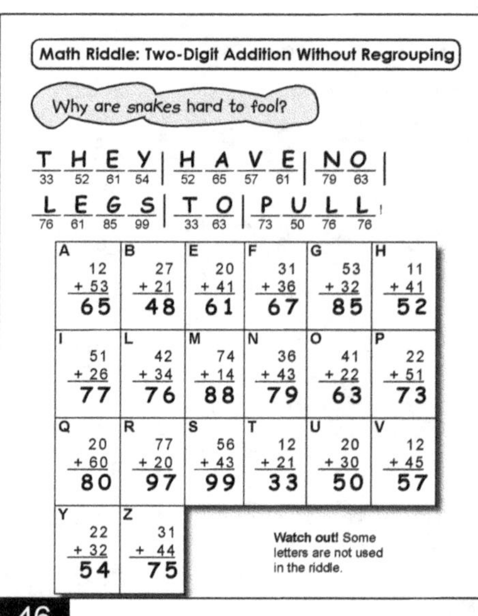

A 12 + 53 = 65	**B** 27 + 21 = 48	**E** 20 + 41 = 61	**F** 31 + 36 = 67	**G** 53 + 32 = 85	**H** 11 + 41 = 52
I 51 + 26 = 77	**L** 42 + 34 = 76	**M** 74 + 14 = 88	**N** 36 + 43 = 79	**O** 41 + 22 = 63	**P** 22 + 51 = 73
Q 20 + 60 = 80	**R** 77 + 20 = 97	**S** 56 + 43 = 99	**T** 12 + 21 = 33	**U** 20 + 30 = 50	**V** 12 + 45 = 57
Y 22 + 32 = 54	**Z** 31 + 44 = 75				

Watch out! Some letters are not used in the riddle.

47 — Two-Digit Addition with Regrouping

Line up the ones and the tens.
Add the ones.
If there are more than 9 ones, trade 10 ones for 1 ten.
Regroup in the tens column.
Write the ones. Then write the tens.

Trade 10 ones from 12 for 1 ten.
Regroup by writing 1 in the tens column.

Use a tens and ones chart to add. Shade the ones column yellow.
Shade the tens column orange.

64 + 18 = 82	22 + 19 = 41	45 + 27 = 72	39 + 22 = 61	49 + 38 = 87
12 + 58 = 70	76 + 14 = 90	64 + 17 = 81	29 + 33 = 62	36 + 36 = 72
54 + 17 = 71	35 + 26 = 61	25 + 25 = 50	62 + 18 = 80	17 + 27 = 44

48 — Two-Digit Addition with Regrouping

Use a tens and ones chart to add. Shade the ones column yellow.
Shade the tens column orange.

17 + 55 = 72	78 + 19 = 97	64 + 16 = 80	57 + 14 = 71	35 + 19 = 54
56 + 38 = 94	24 + 26 = 50	43 + 29 = 72	27 + 66 = 93	48 + 38 = 86
47 + 19 = 66	17 + 48 = 65	34 + 19 = 53	39 + 31 = 70	55 + 26 = 81
59 + 23 = 82	39 + 28 = 67	57 + 16 = 73	64 + 27 = 91	16 + 38 = 54
74 + 18 = 92	57 + 29 = 86	62 + 28 = 90	19 + 39 = 58	29 + 36 = 65

49 — Two-Digit Addition with Regrouping

Use a tens and ones chart to add. Shade the ones column yellow.
Shade the tens column orange.

58 + 24 = 82	44 + 39 = 83	22 + 38 = 60	36 + 47 = 83	47 + 39 = 86
39 + 34 = 73	12 + 49 = 61	55 + 38 = 93	18 + 54 = 72	38 + 38 = 76
63 + 28 = 91	27 + 14 = 41	45 + 46 = 91	65 + 27 = 92	19 + 19 = 38
19 + 78 = 97	46 + 38 = 84	29 + 45 = 74	26 + 66 = 92	76 + 17 = 93
18 + 14 = 32	17 + 43 = 60	35 + 19 = 54	27 + 27 = 54	28 + 45 = 73

50 — Two-Digit Addition with Regrouping

Use a tens and ones chart to add. Shade the ones column yellow.
Shade the tens column orange.

75 + 9 = 84	32 + 38 = 70	55 + 17 = 72	61 + 29 = 90	22 + 8 = 30
48 + 38 = 86	38 + 45 = 83	29 + 69 = 98	29 + 54 = 83	46 + 46 = 92
17 + 57 = 74	13 + 79 = 92	37 + 36 = 73	58 + 29 = 87	45 + 17 = 62
26 + 28 = 54	55 + 39 = 94	35 + 35 = 70	27 + 67 = 94	76 + 5 = 81
37 + 43 = 80	19 + 23 = 42	54 + 38 = 92	38 + 19 = 57	24 + 27 = 51

51 — Math Riddle: Two-Digit Addition with Regrouping

Why did the farmer name his pig Ink?

B E C A U S E | H E
91 62 41 40 47 46 62 | 52 62

K E P T | R U N N I N G |
71 62 43 70 | 61 71 94 94 66 94 63

O U T | O F | H I S | P E N .
93 47 70 | 93 65 | 52 66 46 | 43 62 94

A 17 + 23 = 40	**B** 36 + 55 = 91	**C** 22 + 19 = 41	**D** 37 + 36 = 73	**E** 29 + 33 = 62	**F** 26 + 39 = 65
G 44 + 19 = 63	**H** 29 + 23 = 52	**I** 38 + 28 = 66	**J** 29 + 49 = 78	**K** 59 + 12 = 71	**L** 29 + 28 = 57
N 67 + 27 = 94	**O** 48 + 45 = 93	**P** 29 + 14 = 43	**R** 26 + 35 = 61	**S** 27 + 19 = 46	**T** 35 + 35 = 70
U 18 + 29 = 47	**V** 57 + 27 = 84				

Watch out! Some letters are not used in the riddle.

52 — Math Riddle: Two-Digit Addition with Regrouping

Why was the broom late?

I T | O V E R | S W E P T .
81 51 | 73 70 36 80 | 55 92 36 84 51

Watch out! Some letters are not used in the riddle.

A 14 + 28 = 42	**B** 13 + 49 = 62	**C** 39 + 11 = 50	**D** 38 + 8 = 46	**E** 19 + 17 = 36	**G** 28 + 32 = 60
H 66 + 9 = 75	**I** 63 + 18 = 81	**J** 54 + 7 = 61	**K** 36 + 58 = 94	**L** 48 + 9 = 57	**M** 59 + 19 = 78
N 57 + 6 = 63	**O** 24 + 49 = 73	**P** 57 + 27 = 84	**R** 34 + 46 = 80	**S** 28 + 27 = 55	**T** 16 + 35 = 51
U 49 + 42 = 91	**V** 35 + 35 = 70	**W** 66 + 26 = 92	**X** 19 + 76 = 95	**Y** 77 + 13 = 90	**Z** 24 + 47 = 71

53 — Math Riddle: Two-Digit Addition with Regrouping

Why don't traffic lights go swimming?

B E C A U S E | T H E Y | T A K E | T O O |
92 70 38 20 73 55 70 | 61 71 70 84 | 61 20 60 70 | 81 42 42

L O N G | T O | C H A N G E .
52 42 41 83 | 61 42 | 38 71 20 41 83 70

Watch out! Some letters are not used in the riddle.

A 19 + 1 = 20	**B** 63 + 29 = 92	**C** 29 + 9 = 38	**D** 74 + 19 = 93	**E** 45 + 25 = 70	**F** 69 + 18 = 87
G 58 + 25 = 83	**H** 57 + 14 = 71	**I** 45 + 36 = 81	**J** 78 + 8 = 86	**K** 34 + 26 = 60	**L** 26 + 26 = 52
M 43 + 7 = 50	**N** 28 + 13 = 41	**O** 35 + 7 = 42	**P** 47 + 47 = 94	**Q** 86 + 9 = 95	**R** 35 + 39 = 74
S 39 + 16 = 55	**T** 52 + 9 = 61	**U** 66 + 7 = 73	**V** 17 + 18 = 35	**W** 58 + 32 = 90	**Y** 67 + 17 = 84

54 — Three-Digit Addition Without Regrouping

Line up the ones, tens, and hundreds. Add the ones. Next add the tens. Then add the hundreds.

Use a hundreds, tens, and ones chart to add. Shade the ones column yellow. Shade the tens column orange. Shade the hundreds column green.

454 + 231 = 685	122 + 515 = 637	371 + 327 = 698	135 + 762 = 897
412 + 550 = 962	723 + 225 = 948	462 + 223 = 685	284 + 311 = 595
154 + 833 = 987	231 + 426 = 657	553 + 311 = 864	762 + 137 = 899

Three-Digit Addition Without Regrouping

Use a hundreds, tens, and ones chart to add. Shade the ones column yellow. Shade the tens column orange. Shade the hundreds column green.

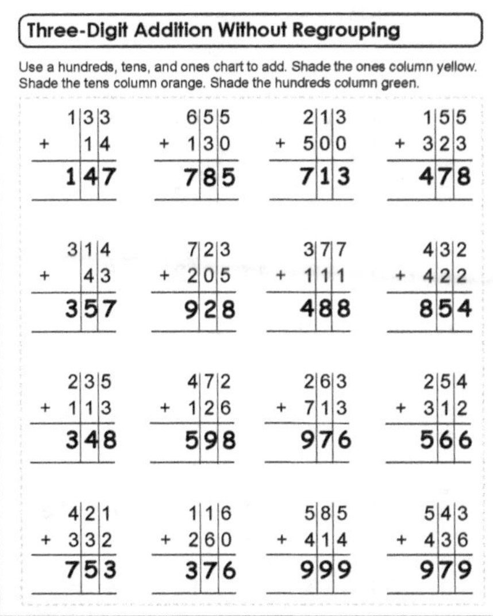

133 + 14 = 147	655 + 130 = 785	213 + 500 = 713	155 + 323 = 478
314 + 43 = 357	723 + 205 = 928	377 + 111 = 488	432 + 422 = 854
235 + 113 = 348	472 + 126 = 598	263 + 713 = 976	254 + 312 = 566
421 + 332 = 753	116 + 260 = 376	585 + 414 = 999	543 + 436 = 979

55

Math Riddle: Three-Digit Addition Without Regrouping

Why did the reporter walk into the ice cream shop?

B E C A U S E | H E | W A N T E D | A
469 359 566 358 243 586 359 | 189 359 | 317 358 697 669 359 337 | 358

S C O O P !
586 566 538 538 956

Watch out! Some letters are not used in the riddle.

A 121 + 237 = 358	B 123 + 346 = 469	C 134 + 432 = 566	D 212 + 125 = 337	E 246 + 113 = 359	F 255 + 524 = 779
H 152 + 37 = 189	I 313 + 154 = 467	J 266 + 112 = 378	K 155 + 341 = 496	L 171 + 528 = 699	M 284 + 215 = 499
N 516 + 181 = 697	O 321 + 217 = 538	P 524 + 432 = 956	Q 435 + 204 = 639	R 112 + 352 = 464	S 443 + 143 = 586
T 253 + 416 = 669	U 142 + 101 = 243	V 564 + 223 = 787	W 305 + 12 = 317	X 171 + 321 = 492	Y 416 + 120 = 536

56

Three-Digit Addition with Regrouping

Line up the ones, tens, and hundreds.
Add the ones.
Then add the tens.

If there are more than 9 tens, trade 10 tens for 1 hundred. Regroup in the hundreds column. Write the tens. Add the hundreds.

Trade 10 tens from 120 for 1 hundred. Regroup by writing 1 in the hundreds column.

Use a hundreds, tens, and ones chart to add. Shade the ones column yellow. Shade the tens column orange. Shade the hundreds column green.

564 + 255 = 819	222 + 491 = 713	175 + 216 = 391	439 + 290 = 729
212 + 195 = 407	376 + 441 = 817	564 + 271 = 835	429 + 180 = 609

57

Three-Digit Addition with Regrouping

Use a hundreds, tens, and ones chart to add. Hint: If there are more than 9 ones, trade 10 ones for 1 ten. Regroup in the tens column.

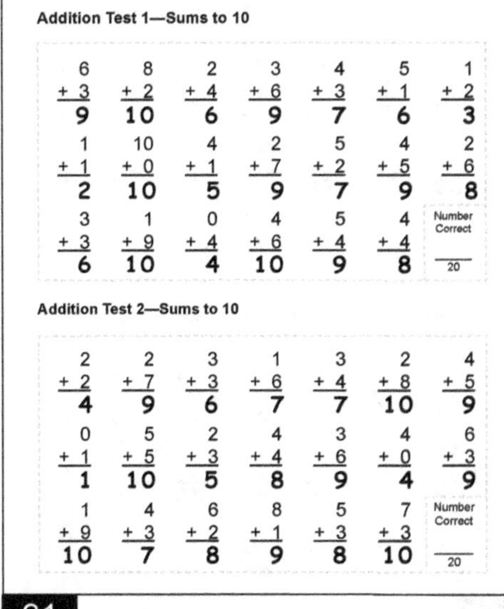

239 + 412 = 651	378 + 319 = 697	464 + 216 = 680	657 + 154 = 811
236 + 398 = 634	824 + 86 = 910	583 + 289 = 872	777 + 164 = 941

Add. Regroup in the tens column and the hundreds column.

379 + 23 = 402	287 + 128 = 415	457 + 166 = 623	564 + 257 = 821

58

Math Riddle: Three-Digit Addition with Regrouping

How do you catch a squirrel?

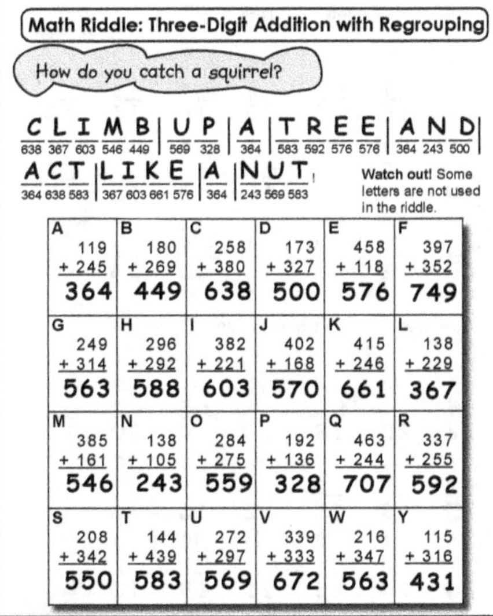

C L I M B | U P | A | T R E E | A N D
638 387 603 546 449 | 569 328 | 364 | 583 592 576 576 | 364 243 500

A C T | L I K E | A | N U T .
364 638 583 | 367 603 661 576 | 364 | 243 569 583

Watch out! Some letters are not used in the riddle.

A 119 + 245 = 364	B 180 + 269 = 449	C 258 + 380 = 638	D 173 + 327 = 500	E 458 + 118 = 576	F 397 + 352 = 749
G 249 + 314 = 563	H 296 + 292 = 588	I 382 + 221 = 603	J 402 + 168 = 570	K 415 + 246 = 661	L 138 + 229 = 367
M 385 + 161 = 546	N 138 + 105 = 243	O 284 + 275 = 559	P 192 + 136 = 328	Q 463 + 244 = 707	R 337 + 255 = 592
S 208 + 342 = 550	T 144 + 439 = 583	U 272 + 297 = 569	V 339 + 333 = 672	W 216 + 347 = 563	Y 115 + 316 = 431

59

Math Riddle: Three-Digit Addition with Regrouping

Why did the student eat his homework?

Watch out! Some letters are not used in the riddle.

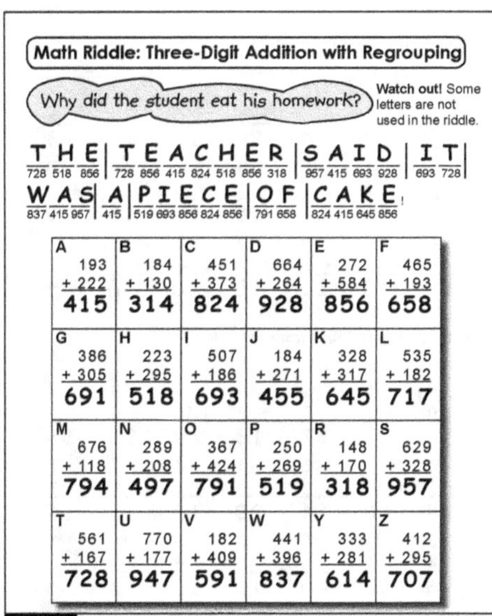

T H E | T E A C H E R | S A I D | I T
728 518 856 | 728 856 415 824 518 856 318 | 957 415 693 928 | 693 728

W A S | A | P I E C E | O F | C A K E .
837 415 957 | 415 | 519 693 856 824 856 | 791 658 | 824 415 645 856

A 193 + 222 = 415	B 184 + 130 = 314	C 451 + 373 = 824	D 664 + 264 = 928	E 272 + 584 = 856	F 465 + 193 = 658
G 386 + 305 = 691	H 223 + 295 = 518	I 507 + 186 = 693	J 184 + 271 = 455	K 328 + 317 = 645	L 535 + 182 = 717
M 676 + 118 = 794	N 289 + 208 = 497	O 367 + 424 = 791	P 250 + 269 = 519	R 148 + 170 = 318	S 629 + 328 = 957
T 561 + 167 = 728	U 770 + 177 = 947	V 182 + 409 = 591	W 441 + 396 = 837	Y 333 + 281 = 614	Z 412 + 295 = 707

60

Addition Test 1—Sums to 10

6 + 3 = 9	8 + 2 = 10	2 + 4 = 6	3 + 6 = 9	4 + 3 = 7	5 + 1 = 6	1 + 2 = 3
1 + 1 = 2	10 + 0 = 10	4 + 1 = 5	2 + 7 = 9	3 + 4 = 7	4 + 5 = 9	2 + 6 = 8
3 + 3 = 6	1 + 9 = 10	0 + 4 = 4	4 + 6 = 10	5 + 4 = 9	4 + 4 = 8	Number Correct __/20

Addition Test 2—Sums to 10

2 + 2 = 4	2 + 7 = 9	3 + 3 = 6	1 + 6 = 7	3 + 4 = 7	2 + 8 = 10	4 + 5 = 9
0 + 1 = 1	5 + 5 = 10	2 + 3 = 5	4 + 4 = 8	3 + 6 = 9	4 + 0 = 4	6 + 3 = 9
1 + 9 = 10	4 + 3 = 7	6 + 2 = 8	8 + 1 = 9	5 + 3 = 8	7 + 3 = 10	Number Correct __/20

61

Addition Test 3—Sums to 10

3 + 3 = 6	2 + 6 = 8	0 + 9 = 9	3 + 4 = 7	7 + 3 = 10	5 + 1 = 6	4 + 6 = 10
5 + 5 = 10	1 + 9 = 10	2 + 0 = 2	5 + 3 = 8	6 + 3 = 9	0 + 5 = 5	7 + 2 = 9
8 + 2 = 10	1 + 7 = 8	0 + 1 = 1	4 + 3 = 7	3 + 1 = 4	3 + 7 = 10	Number Correct __/20

Addition Test 4—Sums to 10

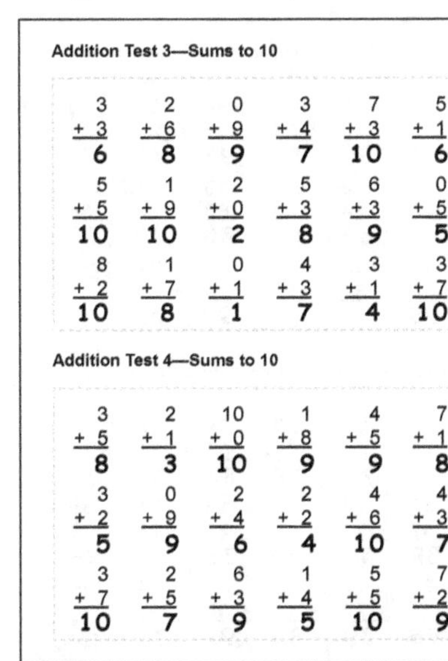

3 + 5 = 8	2 + 1 = 3	10 + 0 = 10	1 + 8 = 9	4 + 5 = 9	7 + 1 = 8	4 + 4 = 8
3 + 2 = 5	0 + 9 = 9	2 + 4 = 6	2 + 2 = 4	4 + 6 = 10	3 + 4 = 7	9 + 1 = 10
3 + 7 = 10	2 + 5 = 7	6 + 3 = 9	1 + 4 = 5	5 + 5 = 10	7 + 2 = 9	Number Correct __/20

62

Addition Test 5—Sums to 10

6 + 3 = 9	8 + 1 = 9	2 + 3 = 5	3 + 6 = 9	4 + 0 = 4	5 + 1 = 6	3 + 2 = 5
1 + 2 = 3	2 + 0 = 2	4 + 1 = 5	1 + 7 = 8	5 + 2 = 7	4 + 6 = 10	2 + 6 = 8
4 + 3 = 7	1 + 9 = 10	0 + 5 = 5	2 + 6 = 8	5 + 4 = 9	2 + 4 = 6	Number Correct __/20

Addition Test 6—Sums to 10

2 + 2 = 4	2 + 6 = 8	0 + 8 = 8	4 + 1 = 5	3 + 0 = 3	2 + 5 = 7	4 + 3 = 7
3 + 4 = 7	7 + 2 = 9	6 + 3 = 9	0 + 6 = 6	4 + 6 = 10	0 + 4 = 4	5 + 3 = 8
1 + 9 = 10	5 + 5 = 10	4 + 4 = 8	8 + 2 = 10	3 + 3 = 6	1 + 1 = ...	Number Correct __/20

63

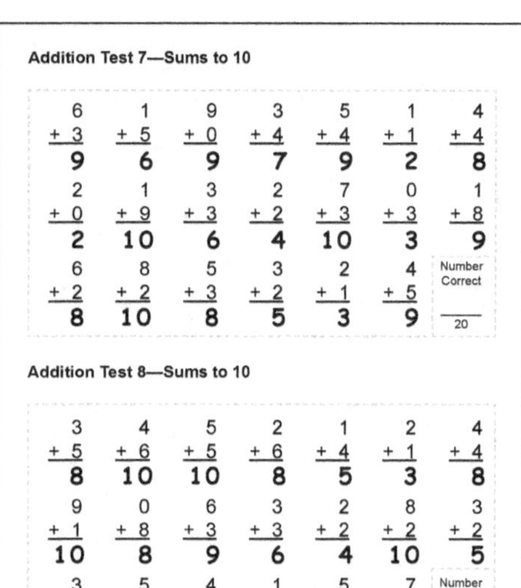

64

Addition Test 7—Sums to 10

6 + 3 = 9	1 + 5 = 6	9 + 0 = 9	3 + 4 = 7	5 + 4 = 9	1 + 1 = 2	4 + 4 = 8
2 + 0 = 2	1 + 9 = 10	3 + 3 = 6	2 + 2 = 4	7 + 3 = 10	0 + 3 = 3	1 + 8 = 9
6 + 2 = 8	8 + 2 = 10	5 + 3 = 8	3 + 2 = 5	2 + 1 = 3	4 + 5 = 9	Number Correct __/20

Addition Test 8—Sums to 10

3 + 5 = 8	4 + 6 = 10	5 + 5 = 10	2 + 6 = 8	1 + 4 = 5	2 + 1 = 3	4 + 4 = 8
9 + 1 = 10	0 + 8 = 8	6 + 3 = 9	3 + 3 = 6	2 + 2 = 4	8 + 2 = 10	3 + 2 = 5
3 + 7 = 10	5 + 2 = 7	4 + 5 = 9	1 + 2 = 3	5 + 4 = 9	7 + 2 = 9	Number Correct __/20

65

Addition Test 9—Sums to 10

2 + 7 = 9	2 + 5 = 7	1 + 2 = 3	3 + 4 = 7	4 + 2 = 6	5 + 5 = 10	3 + 3 = 6
2 + 8 = 10	4 + 4 = 8	6 + 2 = 8	7 + 3 = 10	6 + 3 = 9	1 + 1 = 2	8 + 2 = 10
3 + 2 = 5	0 + 6 = 6	5 + 4 = 9	3 + 5 = 8	4 + 0 = 4	4 + 6 = 10	Number Correct __/20

Addition Test 10—Sums to 10

5 + 3 = 8	4 + 1 = 5	4 + 5 = 9	0 + 2 = 2	3 + 6 = 9	4 + 4 = 8	1 + 0 = 1
0 + 3 = 3	1 + 8 = 9	7 + 2 = 9	3 + 4 = 7	2 + 5 = 7	8 + 2 = 10	3 + 3 = 6
5 + 1 = 6	5 + 2 = 7	3 + 7 = 10	2 + 2 = 4	8 + 1 = 9	7 + 3 = 10	Number Correct __/20

66

Addition Test 1—Sums from 11 to 20

13 + 2 = 15	7 + 7 = 14	3 + 10 = 13	7 + 8 = 15	8 + 6 = 14	6 + 5 = 11	5 + 9 = 14
7 + 5 = 12	8 + 9 = 17	9 + 3 = 12	6 + 9 = 15	17 + 1 = 18	10 + 6 = 16	9 + 10 = 19
10 + 8 = 18	18 + 2 = 20	8 + 4 = 12	5 + 8 = 13	6 + 6 = 12	9 + 7 = 16	Number Correct __/20

Addition Test 2—Sums from 11 to 20

11 + 5 = 16	12 + 6 = 18	10 + 4 = 14	3 + 9 = 12	9 + 9 = 18	6 + 7 = 13	8 + 5 = 13
14 + 2 = 16	5 + 9 = 14	8 + 9 = 17	13 + 5 = 18	11 + 9 = 20	8 + 8 = 16	9 + 4 = 13
10 + 8 = 18	17 + 3 = 20	12 + 3 = 15	5 + 6 = 11	6 + 6 = 12	8 + 6 = 14	Number Correct __/20

67

Addition Test 3—Sums from 11 to 20

13 + 6 = 19	9 + 3 = 12	10 + 4 = 14	12 + 8 = 20	6 + 6 = 12	12 + 3 = 15	7 + 6 = 13
15 + 5 = 20	11 + 2 = 13	16 + 1 = 17	9 + 9 = 18	9 + 5 = 14	10 + 5 = 15	17 + 2 = 19
8 + 9 = 17	9 + 7 = 16	6 + 5 = 11	9 + 6 = 15	14 + 6 = 20	8 + 8 = 16	Number Correct __/20

Addition Test 4—Sums from 11 to 20

6 + 6 = 12	5 + 6 = 11	9 + 8 = 17	10 + 3 = 13	4 + 15 = 19	9 + 9 = 18	7 + 4 = 11
16 + 2 = 18	8 + 10 = 18	5 + 9 = 14	14 + 6 = 20	8 + 4 = 12	7 + 10 = 17	7 + 7 = 14
12 + 4 = 16	13 + 7 = 20	15 + 5 = 20	7 + 9 = 16	9 + 6 = 15	15 + 2 = 17	Number Correct __/20

68

Addition Test 5—Sums from 11 to 20

11 + 9 = 20	8 + 7 = 15	4 + 9 = 13	10 + 8 = 18	9 + 6 = 15	6 + 5 = 11	8 + 6 = 14
5 + 15 = 20	11 + 2 = 13	16 + 4 = 20	9 + 9 = 18	6 + 7 = 13	10 + 5 = 15	17 + 2 = 19
18 + 2 = 20	5 + 7 = 12	10 + 4 = 14	7 + 8 = 15	13 + 2 = 15	7 + 7 = 14	Number Correct __/20

Addition Test 6—Sums from 11 to 20

6 + 6 = 12	13 + 7 = 20	16 + 2 = 18	10 + 3 = 13	14 + 5 = 19	19 + 1 = 20	9 + 2 = 11
13 + 2 = 15	9 + 10 = 19	6 + 9 = 15	7 + 5 = 12	8 + 8 = 16	6 + 10 = 16	9 + 9 = 18
16 + 4 = 20	11 + 3 = 14	8 + 5 = 13	7 + 4 = 11	10 + 9 = 19	10 + 2 = 12	Number Correct __/20

69

Addition Test 7—Sums from 11 to 20

2 + 9 = 11	8 + 7 = 15	17 + 2 = 19	10 + 8 = 18	9 + 6 = 15	6 + 5 = 11	15 + 3 = 18
5 + 8 = 13	11 + 9 = 20	16 + 1 = 17	9 + 9 = 18	6 + 7 = 13	10 + 5 = 15	4 + 8 = 12
8 + 8 = 16	5 + 7 = 12	10 + 4 = 14	7 + 8 = 15	13 + 7 = 20	7 + 7 = 14	Number Correct __/20

Addition Test 8—Sums from 11 to 20

11 + 5 = 16	6 + 8 = 14	9 + 2 = 11	17 + 3 = 20	14 + 5 = 19	9 + 7 = 16	13 + 6 = 19
10 + 2 = 12	6 + 6 = 12	8 + 9 = 17	4 + 10 = 14	4 + 8 = 12	7 + 10 = 17	4 + 7 = 11
13 + 4 = 17	12 + 8 = 20	3 + 9 = 12	7 + 9 = 16	8 + 3 = 11	15 + 2 = 17	Number Correct __/20

70

Addition Test 9—Sums from 11 to 20

2 + 10 = 12	8 + 8 = 16	19 + 1 = 20	10 + 5 = 15	4 + 8 = 12	6 + 5 = 11	5 + 7 = 12
5 + 15 = 20	11 + 2 = 13	16 + 1 = 17	9 + 2 = 11	4 + 7 = 11	9 + 5 = 14	17 + 2 = 19
3 + 9 = 12	9 + 6 = 15	10 + 8 = 18	16 + 4 = 20	13 + 2 = 15	8 + 5 = 13	Number Correct __/20

Addition Test 10—Sums from 11 to 20

7 + 6 = 13	15 + 5 = 20	12 + 8 = 20	20 + 0 = 20	4 + 7 = 11	8 + 6 = 14	14 + 2 = 16
13 + 5 = 18	6 + 10 = 16	9 + 9 = 18	12 + 4 = 16	8 + 3 = 11	7 + 7 = 14	11 + 7 = 18
14 + 4 = 18	10 + 1 = 11	8 + 5 = 13	9 + 7 = 16	6 + 6 = 12	15 + 4 = 19	Number Correct __/20

71

Addition Test 1—Two-Digit Addition Without Regrouping

61 + 24 = 85	72 + 15 = 87	40 + 59 = 99	63 + 24 = 87	84 + 13 = 97	55 + 21 = 76	30 + 42 = 72
14 + 61 = 75	16 + 73 = 89	42 + 44 = 86	34 + 23 = 57	20 + 60 = 80	40 + 42 = 82	33 + 56 = 89
75 + 24 = 99	16 + 82 = 98	55 + 32 = 87	11 + 66 = 77	80 + 19 = 99	27 + 60 = 87	Number Correct __/20

Addition Test 2—Two-Digit Addition Without Regrouping

55 + 34 = 89	72 + 13 = 85	30 + 42 = 72	23 + 55 = 78	54 + 34 = 88	46 + 31 = 77	26 + 12 = 38
41 + 48 = 89	32 + 57 = 89	20 + 37 = 57	35 + 44 = 79	16 + 22 = 38	21 + 78 = 99	35 + 63 = 98
26 + 23 = 49	72 + 24 = 96	17 + 72 = 89	21 + 17 = 38	60 + 39 = 99	14 + 64 = 78	Number Correct __/20

72

Addition Test 3—Two-Digit Addition Without Regrouping

10 + 64 = 74	82 + 17 = 99	20 + 69 = 89	13 + 74 = 87	24 + 33 = 57	45 + 54 = 99	16 + 43 = 59
30 + 59 = 89	10 + 10 = 20	16 + 82 = 98	13 + 25 = 38	40 + 49 = 89	10 + 39 = 49	11 + 58 = 69
47 + 31 = 78	13 + 13 = 26	24 + 40 = 64	15 + 73 = 88	52 + 26 = 78	38 + 61 = 99	Number Correct __/20

Addition Test 4—Two-Digit Addition Without Regrouping

38 + 20 = 58	82 + 17 = 99	37 + 61 = 98	23 + 74 = 97	34 + 34 = 68	49 + 50 = 99	13 + 73 = 86
55 + 44 = 99	16 + 23 = 39	30 + 55 = 85	26 + 23 = 49	10 + 16 = 26	40 + 49 = 89	14 + 52 = 66
83 + 11 = 94	60 + 28 = 88	31 + 37 = 68	12 + 86 = 98	35 + 44 = 79	16 + 62 = 78	Number Correct __/20

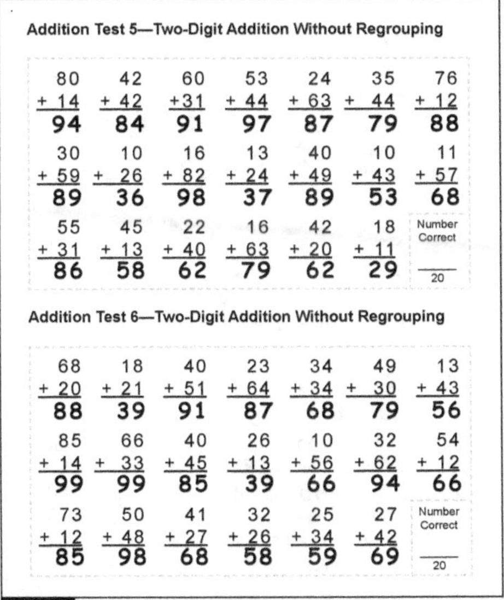

Addition Test 5—Two-Digit Addition Without Regrouping

80 +14 = 94	42 +42 = 84	60 +31 = 91	53 +44 = 97	24 +63 = 87	35 +44 = 79	76 +12 = 88
30 +59 = 89	10 +26 = 36	16 +82 = 98	13 +24 = 37	40 +49 = 89	10 +43 = 53	11 +57 = 68
55 +31 = 86	45 +13 = 58	22 +40 = 62	16 +63 = 79	42 +20 = 62	18 +11 = 29	Number Correct __/20

Addition Test 6—Two-Digit Addition Without Regrouping

68 +20 = 88	18 +21 = 39	40 +51 = 91	23 +64 = 87	34 +34 = 68	49 +30 = 79	13 +43 = 56
85 +14 = 99	66 +33 = 99	40 +45 = 85	26 +13 = 39	10 +56 = 66	32 +62 = 94	54 +12 = 66
73 +12 = 85	50 +48 = 98	41 +27 = 68	32 +26 = 58	25 +34 = 59	27 +42 = 69	Number Correct __/20

73

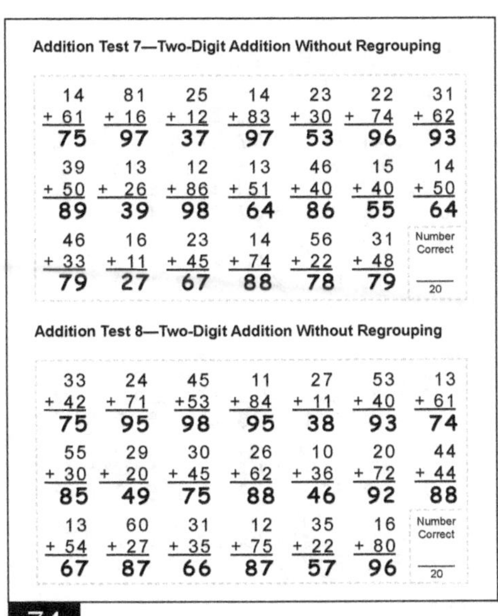

Addition Test 7—Two-Digit Addition Without Regrouping

14 +61 = 75	81 +16 = 97	25 +12 = 37	14 +83 = 97	23 +30 = 53	22 +74 = 96	31 +62 = 93
39 +50 = 89	13 +26 = 39	12 +86 = 98	13 +51 = 64	46 +40 = 86	15 +40 = 55	14 +50 = 64
46 +33 = 79	16 +11 = 27	23 +45 = 67	14 +74 = 88	56 +22 = 78	31 +48 = 79	Number Correct __/20

Addition Test 8—Two-Digit Addition Without Regrouping

33 +42 = 75	24 +71 = 95	45 +53 = 98	11 +84 = 95	27 +11 = 38	53 +40 = 93	13 +61 = 74
55 +30 = 85	29 +20 = 49	30 +45 = 75	26 +62 = 88	10 +36 = 46	20 +72 = 92	44 +44 = 88
13 +54 = 67	60 +27 = 87	31 +35 = 66	12 +75 = 87	35 +22 = 57	16 +80 = 96	Number Correct __/20

74

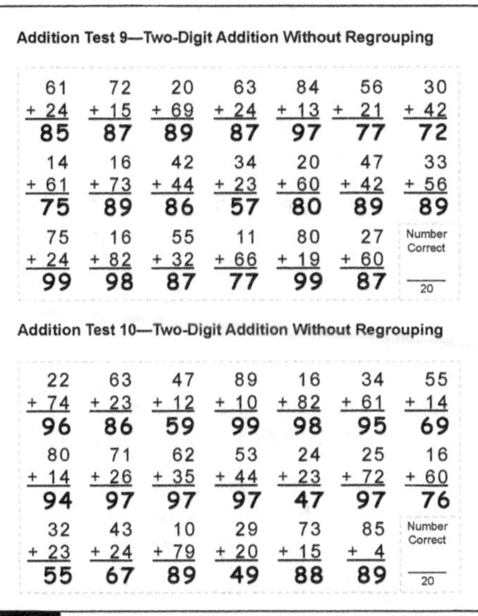

Addition Test 9—Two-Digit Addition Without Regrouping

61 +24 = 85	72 +15 = 87	20 +69 = 89	63 +24 = 87	84 +13 = 97	56 +21 = 77	30 +42 = 72
14 +61 = 75	16 +73 = 89	42 +44 = 86	34 +23 = 57	20 +60 = 80	47 +42 = 89	33 +56 = 89
75 +24 = 99	16 +82 = 98	55 +32 = 87	11 +66 = 77	80 +19 = 99	27 +60 = 87	Number Correct __/20

Addition Test 10—Two-Digit Addition Without Regrouping

22 +74 = 96	63 +23 = 86	47 +12 = 59	89 +10 = 99	16 +82 = 98	34 +61 = 95	55 +14 = 69
80 +14 = 94	71 +26 = 97	62 +35 = 97	53 +44 = 97	24 +23 = 47	25 +72 = 97	16 +60 = 76
32 +23 = 55	43 +24 = 67	10 +79 = 89	29 +20 = 49	73 +15 = 88	85 +4 = 89	Number Correct __/20

75

Addition Test 1—Two-Digit Addition with Regrouping

48 +36 = 84	77 +18 = 95	26 +16 = 42	16 +75 = 91	48 +49 = 97	49 +44 = 93	17 +47 = 64
22 +28 = 50	47 +34 = 81	17 +27 = 44	33 +39 = 72	17 +44 = 61	31 +59 = 90	16 +27 = 43
46 +27 = 73	14 +19 = 33	16 +54 = 70	15 +67 = 82	43 +28 = 71	18 +66 = 84	Number Correct __/20

Addition Test 2—Two-Digit Addition with Regrouping

35 +47 = 82	68 +5 = 73	44 +29 = 73	19 +38 = 57	35 +57 = 92	66 +17 = 83	46 +29 = 75
38 +8 = 46	63 +19 = 82	35 +55 = 90	49 +26 = 75	74 +17 = 91	69 +19 = 88	14 +57 = 71
26 +66 = 92	17 +56 = 73	11 +39 = 50	18 +67 = 85	54 +27 = 81	25 +68 = 93	Number Correct __/20

76

Addition Test 3—Two-Digit Addition with Regrouping

37 +54 = 91	66 +17 = 83	29 +59 = 88	47 +44 = 91	24 +29 = 53	45 +39 = 84	6 +78 = 84
36 +59 = 95	18 +25 = 43	16 +67 = 83	13 +9 = 22	45 +47 = 92	17 +48 = 65	11 +59 = 70
47 +36 = 83	18 +18 = 36	29 +41 = 70	17 +73 = 90	55 +36 = 91	38 +42 = 80	Number Correct __/20

Addition Test 4—Two-Digit Addition with Regrouping

38 +26 = 64	73 +17 = 90	65 +29 = 94	44 +46 = 90	37 +34 = 71	49 +22 = 71	13 +78 = 91
35 +45 = 80	19 +24 = 43	33 +58 = 91	24 +57 = 81	15 +16 = 31	46 +49 = 95	17 +56 = 73
79 +11 = 90	67 +28 = 95	39 +39 = 78	18 +47 = 65	35 +46 = 81	18 +62 = 80	Number Correct __/20

77

Addition Test 5—Two-Digit Addition with Regrouping

55 +37 = 92	87 +7 = 94	54 +18 = 72	7 +67 = 74	64 +19 = 83	45 +25 = 70	48 +23 = 71
56 +39 = 95	27 +49 = 76	76 +18 = 94	24 +36 = 60	49 +43 = 92	15 +55 = 70	19 +51 = 70
47 +36 = 83	48 +44 = 92	29 +51 = 80	18 +63 = 81	37 +53 = 90	29 +42 = 71	Number Correct __/20

Addition Test 6—Two-Digit Addition with Regrouping

58 +26 = 84	77 +13 = 90	49 +24 = 73	26 +45 = 71	37 +36 = 73	28 +58 = 86	13 +79 = 92
56 +26 = 82	29 +23 = 52	55 +39 = 94	36 +34 = 70	17 +27 = 44	18 +44 = 62	59 +26 = 85
85 +9 = 94	63 +28 = 91	17 +36 = 53	38 +47 = 85	65 +6 = 71	18 +62 = 80	Number Correct __/20

78

Addition Test 7—Two-Digit Addition with Regrouping

45 +36 = 81	38 +57 = 95	2 +59 = 61	67 +24 = 91	89 +6 = 95	46 +49 = 95	72 +18 = 90
24 +59 = 83	37 +29 = 66	14 +78 = 92	43 +47 = 90	15 +49 = 64	49 +19 = 68	68 +13 = 81
47 +36 = 83	18 +18 = 36	29 +41 = 70	17 +73 = 90	55 +36 = 91	38 +42 = 80	Number Correct __/20

Addition Test 8—Two-Digit Addition with Regrouping

38 +26 = 64	73 +17 = 90	65 +29 = 94	44 +46 = 90	34 +38 = 72	49 +23 = 72	17 +75 = 92
46 +45 = 91	22 +29 = 51	38 +58 = 96	57 +29 = 86	68 +16 = 84	74 +9 = 83	19 +55 = 74
77 +18 = 95	88 +8 = 96	9 +49 = 58	17 +28 = 45	36 +36 = 72	19 +42 = 61	Number Correct __/20

79

Addition Test 9—Two-Digit Addition with Regrouping

32 +18 = 50	66 +17 = 83	29 +59 = 88	47 +44 = 91	24 +67 = 91	45 +39 = 84	16 +78 = 94
36 +55 = 91	17 +29 = 46	16 +56 = 72	13 +79 = 92	45 +47 = 92	17 +46 = 63	13 +57 = 70
47 +36 = 83	18 +18 = 36	29 +41 = 70	17 +73 = 90	56 +36 = 92	38 +42 = 80	Number Correct __/20

Addition Test 10—Two-Digit Addition with Regrouping

44 +26 = 70	77 +17 = 94	31 +49 = 80	84 +7 = 91	76 +16 = 92	9 +65 = 74	26 +39 = 65
35 +45 = 80	19 +29 = 48	33 +58 = 91	24 +29 = 53	15 +16 = 31	49 +46 = 95	17 +56 = 73
49 +11 = 60	67 +28 = 95	39 +39 = 78	18 +67 = 85	35 +46 = 81	18 +63 = 81	Number Correct __/20

80

Addition Test 1—Three-Digit Addition Without Regrouping

301 +304 = 605	372 +115 = 487	410 +569 = 979	163 +524 = 687	180 +115 = 295	205 +211 = 416	131 +741 = 872
814 +161 = 975	216 +673 = 889	742 +144 = 886	234 +723 = 957	820 +160 = 980	340 +342 = 682	333 +156 = 489
275 +204 = 479	113 +180 = 293	555 +432 = 987	211 +160 = 371	180 +319 = 499	222 +613 = 835	Number Correct __/20

Addition Test 2—Three-Digit Addition Without Regrouping

505 +240 = 745	272 +713 = 985	120 +422 = 542	235 +151 = 386	851 +135 = 986	246 +431 = 677	211 +120 = 331
411 +438 = 849	300 +532 = 832	200 +317 = 517	365 +404 = 769	316 +322 = 638	201 +718 = 919	305 +603 = 908
422 +240 = 662	732 +244 = 976	125 +271 = 396	131 +107 = 238	610 +349 = 959	140 +654 = 794	Number Correct __/20

81

Addition Test 3—Three-Digit Addition Without Regrouping

110 + 604 = 714	820 + 127 = 947	320 + 615 = 935	313 + 114 = 427	254 + 313 = 567	425 + 554 = 979	186 + 403 = 589
130 + 549 = 679	790 + 100 = 890	116 + 182 = 298	123 + 250 = 373	400 + 469 = 869	120 + 361 = 481	117 + 860 = 977
147 + 341 = 488	103 + 133 = 236	124 + 740 = 864	715 + 273 = 988	652 + 126 = 778	130 + 160 = 290	Number Correct __/20

Addition Test 4—Three-Digit Addition Without Regrouping

380 + 200 = 580	420 + 117 = 537	307 + 651 = 958	203 + 794 = 997	835 + 130 = 965	349 + 250 = 599	615 + 371 = 986
500 + 470 = 970	112 + 230 = 342	730 + 255 = 985	211 + 280 = 491	180 + 106 = 286	494 + 400 = 894	314 + 532 = 846
283 + 110 = 393	160 + 128 = 288	314 + 130 = 444	112 + 826 = 938	301 + 412 = 713	160 + 632 = 792	

82

Addition Test 5—Three-Digit Addition Without Regrouping

150 + 100 = 250	192 + 402 = 594	210 + 731 = 941	253 + 244 = 497	124 + 663 = 787	305 + 434 = 739	700 + 112 = 812
333 + 530 = 863	160 + 126 = 286	611 + 280 = 891	213 + 724 = 937	140 + 435 = 575	210 + 432 = 642	131 + 527 = 658
505 + 391 = 896	454 + 140 = 594	122 + 401 = 523	316 + 163 = 479	142 + 250 = 392	118 + 111 = 229	Number Correct __/20

Addition Test 6—Three-Digit Addition Without Regrouping

618 + 120 = 738	217 + 220 = 437	340 + 531 = 871	231 + 604 = 835	131 + 340 = 471	249 + 300 = 549	713 + 243 = 956
850 + 149 = 999	653 + 330 = 983	430 + 245 = 675	126 + 813 = 939	101 + 567 = 668	320 + 622 = 942	542 + 100 = 642
703 + 122 = 825	500 + 441 = 941	141 + 211 = 352	342 + 246 = 588	206 + 310 = 516	201 + 142 = 343	Number Correct __/20

83

Addition Test 7—Three-Digit Addition Without Regrouping

114 + 601 = 715	821 + 126 = 947	253 + 132 = 385	144 + 423 = 567	523 + 350 = 873	227 + 742 = 969	310 + 602 = 912
339 + 350 = 689	132 + 260 = 392	210 + 681 = 891	113 + 251 = 364	546 + 440 = 986	105 + 400 = 505	114 + 150 = 264
476 + 313 = 789	618 + 160 = 778	222 + 452 = 674	314 + 374 = 688	356 + 232 = 588	331 + 103 = 434	

Addition Test 8—Three-Digit Addition Without Regrouping

313 + 402 = 715	233 + 711 = 944	452 + 523 = 975	111 + 243 = 354	427 + 141 = 563	453 + 410 = 863	510 + 361 = 871
305 + 350 = 655	296 + 600 = 896	360 + 125 = 485	261 + 621 = 882	101 + 236 = 337	220 + 742 = 962	468 + 410 = 878
100 + 154 = 254	680 + 217 = 897	231 + 235 = 466	512 + 375 = 887	235 + 242 = 477	160 + 330 = 490	Number Correct __/20

84

Addition Test 9—Three-Digit Addition Without Regrouping

761 + 124 = 885	692 + 105 = 797	220 + 629 = 849	262 + 210 = 472	834 + 133 = 967	540 + 251 = 791	230 + 542 = 772
214 + 331 = 545	116 + 523 = 639	412 + 474 = 886	314 + 213 = 527	120 + 860 = 980	247 + 642 = 889	323 + 500 = 823
105 + 234 = 339	215 + 110 = 325	651 + 330 = 981	619 + 260 = 879	800 + 109 = 909	207 + 620 = 827	Number Correct __/20

Addition Test 10—Three-Digit Addition Without Regrouping

212 + 774 = 986	603 + 243 = 846	447 + 142 = 589	189 + 210 = 399	605 + 223 = 998	134 + 761 = 895	755 + 114 = 869
860 + 104 = 964	761 + 210 = 971	162 + 835 = 997	203 + 184 = 387	424 + 423 = 847	205 + 792 = 997	112 + 860 = 972
320 + 233 = 553	243 + 124 = 367	110 + 179 = 289	322 + 120 = 442	673 + 215 = 888	130 + 221 = 351	Number Correct __/20

85

Addition Test 1—Three-Digit Addition with Regrouping

197 + 276 = 473	276 + 238 = 514	396 + 266 = 662	436 + 289 = 725	588 + 249 = 837	679 + 246 = 925	787 + 147 = 934
682 + 128 = 810	597 + 132 = 729	496 + 127 = 623	383 + 431 = 814	277 + 354 = 631	152 + 259 = 411	599 + 199 = 798
591 + 221 = 812	494 + 419 = 913	376 + 354 = 730	285 + 268 = 553	343 + 378 = 721	168 + 166 = 334	Number Correct __/20

Addition Test 2—Three-Digit Addition with Regrouping

185 + 257 = 442	267 + 279 = 546	349 + 189 = 538	483 + 438 = 921	594 + 357 = 951	665 + 176 = 841	777 + 129 = 906
736 + 191 = 927	669 + 183 = 852	535 + 271 = 806	449 + 226 = 675	374 + 434 = 808	269 + 549 = 818	184 + 651 = 835
366 + 166 = 532	467 + 256 = 723	391 + 339 = 730	588 + 267 = 855	154 + 657 = 811	222 + 189 = 411	Number Correct __/20

86

Addition Test 3—Three-Digit Addition with Regrouping

331 + 188 = 519	466 + 197 = 663	569 + 59 = 628	148 + 404 = 552	594 + 227 = 821	145 + 689 = 834	776 + 178 = 954
131 + 399 = 530	708 + 129 = 837	216 + 188 = 404	183 + 327 = 510	445 + 489 = 934	286 + 349 = 635	571 + 159 = 730
447 + 236 = 683	398 + 218 = 616	299 + 501 = 800	377 + 473 = 850	252 + 676 = 928	138 + 172 = 310	Number Correct __/20

Addition Test 4—Three-Digit Addition with Regrouping

244 + 191 = 435	377 + 117 = 494	191 + 409 = 600	284 + 517 = 801	171 + 119 = 290	199 + 615 = 814	126 + 499 = 625
155 + 185 = 340	119 + 129 = 248	673 + 58 = 731	174 + 199 = 373	115 + 396 = 511	486 + 489 = 975	267 + 686 = 953
289 + 211 = 500	367 + 328 = 695	439 + 439 = 878	218 + 187 = 405	435 + 346 = 781	518 + 163 = 681	Number Correct __/20

87

Addition Test 5—Three-Digit Addition with Regrouping

688 + 40 = 728	767 + 107 = 874	398 + 315 = 713	87 + 594 = 681	853 + 98 = 951	162 + 777 = 939	537 + 168 = 705
119 + 199 = 318	229 + 189 = 418	648 + 188 = 836	208 + 344 = 552	154 + 489 = 643	91 + 791 = 882	571 + 290 = 861
539 + 235 = 774	661 + 299 = 960	341 + 388 = 729	189 + 142 = 331	224 + 176 = 400	67 + 744 = 811	Number Correct __/20

Addition Test 6—Three-Digit Addition with Regrouping

425 + 191 = 616	340 + 273 = 613	290 + 453 = 743	228 + 417 = 645	533 + 288 = 821	203 + 559 = 762	61 + 459 = 520
106 + 685 = 791	477 + 329 = 806	583 + 58 = 641	663 + 199 = 862	475 + 397 = 872	234 + 199 = 433	899 + 77 = 976
393 + 55 = 448	479 + 489 = 968	690 + 287 = 977	328 + 484 = 812	544 + 346 = 890	185 + 167 = 352	Number Correct __/20

88

Addition Test 7—Three-Digit Addition with Regrouping

582 + 48 = 630	463 + 108 = 571	299 + 375 = 674	386 + 494 = 880	53 + 398 = 451	668 + 77 = 745	439 + 108 = 547
518 + 194 = 712	279 + 188 = 467	248 + 197 = 445	408 + 344 = 752	254 + 489 = 743	82 + 631 = 713	575 + 308 = 883
136 + 236 = 372	377 + 253 = 630	127 + 399 = 526	184 + 147 = 331	253 + 198 = 451	67 + 685 = 752	Number Correct __/20

Addition Test 8—Three-Digit Addition with Regrouping

465 + 261 = 726	380 + 383 = 763	230 + 583 = 813	217 + 697 = 914	596 + 308 = 904	205 + 659 = 864	99 + 889 = 988
106 + 685 = 791	27 + 799 = 826	533 + 188 = 721	643 + 299 = 942	455 + 377 = 832	264 + 168 = 432	748 + 77 = 825
693 + 44 = 737	379 + 591 = 970	590 + 372 = 962	328 + 209 = 537	865 + 46 = 911	289 + 267 = 556	Number Correct __/20

89

Addition Test 9—Three-Digit Addition with Regrouping

779 + 58 = 837	263 + 109 = 372	288 + 545 = 833	345 + 294 = 639	79 + 438 = 517	125 + 89 = 214	869 + 108 = 977
686 + 194 = 880	215 + 188 = 403	224 + 197 = 421	408 + 343 = 751	232 + 489 = 721	41 + 691 = 732	555 + 307 = 862
176 + 232 = 408	379 + 259 = 638	167 + 369 = 536	148 + 184 = 332	254 + 117 = 371	38 + 785 = 823	Number Correct __/20

Addition Test 10—Three-Digit Addition with Regrouping

485 + 381 = 866	360 + 463 = 823	230 + 583 = 813	217 + 607 = 824	596 + 378 = 974	105 + 789 = 894	99 + 881 = 980
626 + 185 = 811	27 + 799 = 826	193 + 588 = 781	153 + 299 = 452	445 + 377 = 822	264 + 168 = 432	778 + 82 = 860
663 + 53 = 716	399 + 298 = 697	580 + 377 = 957	318 + 206 = 524	825 + 45 = 870	239 + 264 = 503	Number Correct __/20

90